**Marshall Cavendish**
Business

To my Granny – Doris Lewis (1912–2006),
who didn't see the point of computers, but would have
approved of the bargains to be found on eBay

Copyright © 2008 Elen Lewis

First published in 2008 by:

Marshall Cavendish Limited
Fifth Floor
32–38 Saffron Hill
London EC1N 8FH
United Kingdom
T: +44 (0)20 7421 8120
F: +44 (0)20 7421 8121
sales@marshallcavendish.co.uk
www.marshallcavendish.co.uk

A CIP record for this book is available from the British Library.

ISBN-10 1-905736-10-X
ISBN-13 978-1-905736-10-2

Illustrations by Jamie Pike

Designed and typeset by Phoenix Photosetting,
Lordswood, Chatham, Kent

Printed and bound in Great Britain by
TJ International Ltd, Padstow, Cornwall

Contents

Acknowledgments

Many different people, all over the world have helped me with the research of this book. Unfortunately, most of them cannot be named as they spoke to me off the record. For my contacts close to and within eBay – thank you. You know who you are.

I'd also like to thank those who shed a light on eBay and auction culture including Richard Rock, Jay Fiore, Alan Mitchell and Jim Rose. Caroline Wiertz was a valuable source of information about online communities. *The Perfect Store* by Adam Cohen was a valuable background read.

A big thank you to my Greek chorus, the many professional eBayers that I met at eBay University or online who helped me tremendously. They were passionate, candid and insightful, and included Andrew and Kirsty from Postalsupplies, Dr Steve W, Jon from Allsorts, Miss Cosmopolitan, Andrew Fischer, Steve Woodward, Chris and Sean Coolness.

Thanks to Martin Liu and Pom Somkabcharti at Cyan Books and series editor John Simmons for their tireless help and support. Thank you to Morag Cuddeford Jones, contributing editor at *Brand Strategy* magazine, who helped set up some essential interviews for the book. I'd also like to thank my mother-in-law Anne Paynter at the Open University for resourcefully helping me with research.

Final big thanks to mum, dad, Tom and Alice, for nurturing the first few chapters in sunny North Wales with the vital ingredients of chocolate digestives, milky tea and walks. And thank you always to Rosie, my daughter, and Simon, my husband, a patient critic, proof reader, DIY miracle office builder, IT helpdesk and lasagne chef. I'm a lucky lady and couldn't have written it without you.

Preface

It seemed unlikely, as the new century came into being, that two of the brands that would soon be ranked among the world's biggest and best would owe their entire existence to the internet. After all, the talk had been of the bursting of the dotcom bubble, and there was the evidence in thousands of examples of failed internet businesses. Yet these two brands spectacularly survived and thrived to such an extent that, in the 2006 Interbrand/Business Week survey, they were both comfortably positioned in the top 50 of the world's most valuable brands. So it is certainly worth examining what has made Google and eBay so successful in such a short time.

Neil Taylor wrote about Google in an earlier book in this series. Now Elen Lewis writes about eBay and she brings qualities of charm, enthusiasm and dogged curiosity to her task. Elen understands and enjoys brands, and there's no doubt that you need to feel an affinity for a brand to write a book in this series. The reason is simple: the task of a brand is to create ties with its audience. You need to understand that by feeling it, by being in tune with the emotion that is engendered by the brand. But you need objectivity and independence too, and Elen was actually helped by the fact that eBay opened no doors to make it easier for her to write this book.

Having been refused official access by eBay, Elen talked to those who would willingly talk to her: the eBay community. In doing so, she was taken to the absolute heart of the brand. EBay succeeds as a brand because it is all about people not technology. Of course, the technology enables the human and commercial interaction to happen, and eBay would not exist without the internet. But the reason why eBay succeeded and countless dotcoms failed is that it struck upon fundamental truths about human behaviour. In doing so, it created a business that spans the world and potentially appeals to every human being on the planet. It's quite an achievement and a great story that Elen Lewis tells.

John Simmons
Series editor, *Great Brand Stories*

Introduction

I like to think it was poetic justice that I received my first eBay
star the week I finished writing this book. It was testament to my
so-called "book research," which probably equates to lots of
money but more importantly, three hooded tops, a stripy pink
jumper, some magnetic letters for my fridge, some feathering
fishing bait for my husband, an amplifier and my favourite
purchase – three vintage bronze letters, a C, I and N. I just need
to collect the rest of the alphabet. And I don't know how I'd find
them without eBay.

The irony of writing a book about eBay is how seductive the subject matter becomes. (Although distracting is a more appropriate word.) In the midst of innocently researching some corporate history, I suddenly find myself frantically bidding against paula276 for an antique chandelier.

I'd hoped that eBay would be interested in co-operating with this book. Unfortunately, they said that eBay was about their community, that they didn't like speaking for them. So I became not an official storyteller but a sleuth.

I loitered outside eBay's headquarters and I approached eBay employees through friends and colleagues. I attended eBay University (twice) undercover. During one session I had three eBay employees sitting around me smiling. I thought it was to stop me talking to other eBayers, but maybe I was getting paranoid. I even auctioned a chapter of this book on eBay.

I was scolded by eBay for inappropriate behaviour in the chat rooms, where I liked to skulk. I was barred from attending eBay Live! in Las Vegas, because, "based on the supporting materials that you provided, you have not met our specified requirements for media/analyst credentials." Strange, it's the first time it's happened during my eleven-year career as a journalist.

So I spoke to the eBay community instead, the buyers and sellers who live and breathe auctions, who tell eBay HQ what to do next. They became my Greek chorus. And like a Greek chorus I suspect they told me a more truthful tale than the official story may have been.

In fact, the deeper into my research I became, the more appropriate I realized it was to grill the chorus, rather than the protagonists of the eBay drama. They do all the hard work – the listing, the packing, the posting, the marketing. Meanwhile, all the eBay officials need to do is provide the arena for them to set up their stalls.

They sang the eBay song to me, they sent me essays they'd written, and they tried to sell me outdoor swimming pools, gardening tools and shoes. And they talked and talked about how eBay had transformed their lives, granted them financial independence, connected them with new friends but also, sometimes, caused them frustration.

In hindsight, I realize that this book is more interesting for its independence. I'm not interested in the corporate line and instead I believe I've glimpsed the organic messiness of a new generation brand: a brand that is less about consistency and more about the involvement of its community.

EBay is a fluid, shifting, keeps-you-on-your-tiptoes kind of brand. Its world changes so swiftly that, by the time you're reading this book, something new will invariably have happened that I haven't been able to document.

The drama that follows delves behind the official eBay mask to reveal the kaleidoscopic, global jumble sale of everyman. It's the story of the agoraphobic shopaholic, the comic book obsessive who finds love and sells his collection, the broken-hearted husband, the wily entrepreneur. Unlike any other brand I know, eBay offers a snapshot of humanity. All human life is there.

Chapter 1
Bid Thee Well

Next Town For sale

November 23 2004

Virgin Mary in Grilled Cheese. NOT A HOAX! LOOK AND SEE!

"I made this sandwich 10 years ago. When I took a bite out of it, I saw a face looking up at me. It was the Virgin Mary. It has preserved itself, which in itself I consider to be a miracle. People ask me if I have had blessings since she has been in my home, I do feel I have."

Imagine strolling through a flea market where you could buy a Gulfstream jet, a Californian gold rush town or a bucket of sea water. Imagine visiting a place where you can be whoever you want to be, where you can tap dance across the floor, even if you can't hear the beat in the real world.

Imagine joining a community where over 200 million perfect strangers have learnt to trust one another, although they've never met. Welcome to a mad, whirling, online souk called eBay. A global jumble sale that is ruled by the thrill of the auction and a brand that has changed the world we live in today.

EBay is a global, online marketplace that has empowered individuals. It has enabled the entrepreneur working from his spare bedroom to trade with millions and millions of buyers from 38 different countries. It has enabled the Chinese seamstress to sell silk pyjamas directly to the urban glitterati in New York and connected PEZ collectors from Canada with their counterparts in the Cook Islands.

EBay has changed our attitude to accumulating and

consuming. Why hoard Great Auntie's ugly antiques in the attic, when we can make a killing by selling them on eBay? The global marketplace has communicated the intoxicating promise that one man's rubbish is another man's treasure.

This promise has created an army of bubble wrap entre-preneurs. Their lives flicker between the glimmering computer screen, where the minutes of their auction tick away, and queuing at the Post Office. EBay is their office, their warehouse, their telephone service, their accounts department and their shop floor.

Temporary ownership is the driving force behind eBay. When viewed through the eBay lens, buying and consuming doesn't have to be a decision weighed down by financial burden. It's the ultimate window shopping, with the pull of the buy-it-now-and-you-won't-regret-it-later-because-you-can-always-sell-it-again mentality.

EBay offers the seductive chance to own a second-hand designer handbag until we get bored of it. It provides the opportunity to clear out our wardrobe, to redesign our bedroom, our house, our hobbies, our life, all by trading online.

Since its launch during the heady dotcom days of the late 1990s, eBay has grown to become one of the biggest global brands, alongside century-old Coca-Cola and Disney. In 2007, eBay's was named the 48th most valuable brand in the world, worth $7.5bn, an increase of 10 percent since the previous year.[1] And you know a brand has made it when it disrupts language – "to eBay" entered the Collins dictionary in June 2005.

It all began one September weekend in Silicon Valley, when computer geek Pierre Omidyar decided to sell his broken laser pointer on a clunky, grey-coloured auction site he'd added to his home page. As interest escalated and the bids accumulated until the broken item was sold at a profit, Omidyar realized that maybe eBay might change the world.

Today, there are 250 million registered eBay users worldwide,

10 times more than the population of Australia. If eBay were a nation, it would be the fifth largest in the world, with only China, India, the US and Indonesia ahead. EBay users trade more than $1,812 worth of goods on the site every second.

TOASTED FAITH

For sale: Virgin Mary Grilled Cheese Sandwich

November 23 2004

Winning bid: $28,000

I made this sandwich 10 years ago, when I took a bite out of it, I saw a face looking up at me, It was Virgin Mary starring back at me, I was in total shock, I would like to point out there is no mold or disingration, The item has not been preserved or anything, It has been keep in a plastic case, not a special one that seals out air or potiental mold or bacteria, it is like a miracle, It has just preserved itself which in itself I consider a miracle, people ask me if I have had blessings since she has been in my home, I do feel I have, I have won $70,000 (total) on different occasions at the casino near by my house. I would like all bidders to know that this item is not intended for consumption, it is intended for collectable purposes only.

THE AUCTIONS OF THE BIZARRE

All human life is here on eBay. In a world ruled by "time remaining," shoppers can buy everything and the kitchen sink with the click of a button. Every day, there are over 102 million live listings on eBay in 50,000 different product categories, with 6 million items added daily. There are cuckoo clocks, camper vans, castanets, comics, cats, corgi cars, and cribs, cross stitch kits, concert tickets, cancer cures and castles.

The most expensive item sold on eBay was a 12-seater Gulfstream II Jet sold for $4.9m in 2001. Since then, Zhang Cheng, a Chinese business man has paid $24,730 for a MiG fighter jet to display outside his company. And in 2005, a silver VW Golf once owned by Pope Benedict XVI reached $244,590, more than 25 times its retail value.

One of the more unusual items to have been sold on eBay is a 50,000-year-old Mammoth called Max. Weighing in at 250,000 kilos, Max was put up for sale in 2005 by his Dutch owner due to lack of space and sold for $115,591. A bargain considering he was one of the five best and most complete mammoth skeletons in the world, with 90 percent of his original bone material.

In 2002, an entire town was sold on eBay for just under $1.8m. Bridgeville, a 130-year old Californian gold rush town, lies 260 miles north of San Francisco. The lot's 82 acres included 10 houses, four cabins and a postcode, although the seller warned: "Be prepared to do a lot of work to get the town into sparkling condition."

SELLING THE POPE MOBILE

For sale: 1999 Volkswagen Golf, once owned by Cardinal Joseph Ratzinger, now Pope Benedict XVI

May 5 2005

227 bids, 8.5 million visitors

Winning bid: $244,590.83

The metallic gray 1999 2.0-liter Golf with 47,000 miles. Unbelievable! This is not an ordinary car. Your driving will always be save and blessed in it. You won't believe it, but the former car-holder was our new Pope, Benedict XVI. The car looks as if it was new due to the care it god. It drives like heaven.

There have been kidneys and souls for sale, a British student's virginity and a decommissioned nuclear bunker. A wedding dress modelled by the bride's ex-husband was viewed by 17 million people, eventually sold for $3,850, and led to three marriage proposals. "Don't worry ladies, I am wearing clothes underneath. I gotta say it did make me feel pretty. I was also told to say it has a veil and a train and all kinds of shiny beads and things," he wrote.

THE MAN WHO MODELLED HIS EX-WIFE'S WEDDING DRESS

For sale: One Slightly Used Size 12 Wedding Gown. Only worn twice: Once at the wedding and once for these pictures.

April 23 2004

113 bids

Winning bid: $3,850.00

I found my ex-wife's wedding dress in the attic when I moved. She took the $4000 engagement ring but left the dress. This dress cost me $1200 that my drunken sot of an ex-father-in-law swore up and down he would pay for but didn't so I got stuck with the bill. Luckily I only got stuck with his daughter for 5 years. Personally, I think it looks like a $1200 shower curtain, but what do I know about this. We tried taking pictures of this lovely white garment but it didn't look right on the hanger. Actually I didn't think my head would fit in the neck hole, but then I figured she got her Texas cheerleader hair through there I could get my head in it. I gotta say it did make me feel very pretty. Anyway, I was told to say it has a train and a veil and all kinds of shiny beady things. Ladies, you won't regret this. You may regret the dude you marry but not the dress. Please only bid if you are serious. Or really, really hot.

EBay has traded the meaning of life, a virtual girlfriend and a time machine, whose listing claimed: "has not been in action for a while, only used thrice, has some rust along the bottom."[2] Then there was the eBayer's son who sold his guardian angel.

And aside from the weird auctions, eBay also trades large volumes of the flotsam and jetsam of everyday life. It sells one car, one laptop and one teddy bear every two minutes.

Ebay Time

A car sells every 2 minutes
A CD sells every 7 seconds
A teddy bear sells every 2 minutes
A toy car sells every 26 seconds
A mobile phone sells every 21 seconds
A laptop sells every 2 minutes
An MP3 player sells every 2 minutes
A woman's handbag sells every 36 seconds
A piece of women's clothing sells every 7 seconds
A piece of men's clothing sells every 13 seconds
A football shirt sells every 5 minutes
A piece of golf equipment sells every 1 minute[3]

BRANDING THE RABBLE

EBay's business model is almost entirely reliant on its army of buyers and sellers. While eBay provides the arena, its community must set up their market stalls, engage their customers and sell them stuff before packing and posting it to them. The only guaranteed winner of eBay's auctions is eBay itself, as it charges traders to sell items on its marketplace and takes a slice of their proceeds.

The members of eBay's vast online community trust each other, although they've never met. This is largely due to a self-regulated ratings system where traders leave feedback for each other following transactions. It means bidders can have confidence that the seller will not take their money and run, while sellers are confident that the winning bidder pays for their item. EBay's 248 million members worldwide have left more than three billion feedback comments for one another regarding their transactions.

EBay's global community are not merely trading partners, they're also friends. Dave and Annie from Derbyshire in the UK got married this summer after meeting at a party for eBay enthusiasts. They had an eBay-themed wedding and bought outfits and paraphernalia on the site. Other traders will talk on the phone, in the chat rooms and meet up at eBay gatherings.

While social networking has reached dizzy new heights thanks to the likes of MySpace, FaceBook and YouTube; eBay has been providing a fertile environment for its community for over 10 years. EBay's members have conversations like the one opposite.

EBay's brand is moulded and guided by its community. It is a brand of the new generation; a brand that is less about consistency and more about involvement and interaction with consumers. It's an organic, messy brand that enables its customers to shout and rage in its chat rooms and rebel against unpopular corporate decisions.

Sometimes, this symbiotic relationship makes life more complicated for eBay's leaders, but when it works, it can result in some of the brand's best innovation. It also means that eBay grows through word-of-mouth and has some of the most loyal consumers in the world. However, since eBay floated on the stock exchange it has become increasingly difficult for management to listen so closely to the community, as it must also please investors.

EBay Round Table Annonimous Meeting

Cheesey69 (1185) begins the chat: *hand in here sobbing* yes i admit it im so ashamed im an ebay addict*sobs in to hanky* ok who wants to start todays meeting? *looks at rest of group*

Fran tasy island (69): *stands slowly and whispers* i have a problem. its this place i go, well not really, it doesnt actually exhist, but i spend alot of time there....oh i cant explain

Speedydub (0): mmm.... and do you spend money and not remember doing it?...strange packages arriving at your house?

Fran tasy island (69): uh huh, yeah then things come to the door..........strange things in boxes or brown envelopes.....with MY name on!

Mfkirke (2269): I have been crying out for this sort of help on my ME page for over a year. In the meantime, my feedback has gone through the roof. My husband can only recognize the back of my head. And the house is full of bubble wrap and polystyrene fill.

EBAY-NOMICS

EBay has changed the face of retail through its empowerment of consumers. The old-fashioned offline world was one where producers said to customers: "I've made this; buy it from me at this price." In eBay's world, consumers are saying, "I want this: sell it to me at this price." The development of online auctions and the potentially level playing field they can create has fascinated many economists.

Classic economic theory teaches us that the auction format can achieve the perfect price because items sell at the exact point where supply met demand. EBay's auctions have helped create efficient markets where they previously didn't work well or perhaps didn't even exist.

In the world of eBay-nomics, small traders can thrive with access to buyers in global markets. When people are given access to markets, they can benefit as producers, not just consumers. EBay has empowered people to give up jobs they hate. Over 170,000 people across Europe rely on eBay for their primary or secondary income and 81 percent of these small businesses employ between one and 10 people, while 29 percent say they plan to hire more staff in the next two years.[4]

In the US, more than 730,000 people make a full-time income from eBay. In the UK, an estimated 50,000 people use eBay to boost their incomes by around £3,000 ($5,684) a year. And eBay is an economy in its own right. The total value of trades was around $34bn in 2005. EBay is the 59th largest economy in the world, just behind Kuwait and growing more rapidly.[5]

The arrival of eBay has tilted the balance of power towards the owners of second-hand goods. They now have a mechanism for advertising, gauging the interest of buyers and maximizing price. They can now feel confident that they're selling goods for their most accurate value.

ATRIUM AUCTIONARIUM

Auctions have touched almost every century, every industry and every nationality. Around 500BC, in the first auctions to be documented by Herodotus in ancient Greece, women were sold as wives. Indeed, at this time it was considered illegal to sell a daughter outside an auction. Records show that less attractive women normally had to provide a dowry, and the winning bidder was often compensated.

The Roman Empire also held auctions in the "atrium auctionarium"; they were popular for selling war plunder and family estates. When Marcus Aurelius was in debt, he sold off family heirlooms and family furniture in an auction that lasted two months.

But the most bizarre early auction, and one that would not look out of place among eBay's marketplace, was that of the entire Roman Empire in AD193. When the Praetorian Guard killed Pertinax, the emperor, they announced the highest bidder could claim the empire. Didius Julianus won, becoming emperor for the price of 6,250 denarii per guard. However, he was beheaded two months later when Septimius Severus conquered Rome.

Less is known about auctions in other ancient civilizations. However, Buddhist temples and monasteries in ancient China used auctions to raise money and build new temples. In the seventh century, records show that the possessions of dead monks were auctioned off.

The earliest modern record of the word auction appeared in 1595, according to the *Oxford English Dictionary,* but it wasn't until the 17th century that auctions were held in taverns and coffeehouses to sell art. And in the following century, the auction houses Sotheby's (1744) and Christie's (1766) were founded.

Auctions were also held in The Netherlands and Germany in the latter part of the 19th century. From 1887, fruit and vegetables were sold in Dutch auctions, while German fishermen used auctions to sell their catch when arriving in port.

THE DOTCOM BOOM

While eBay's business model is powered by the auction, it is inspired by a patchwork of influences, including the Victorian age of collecting and the Marché aux Puces fleamarket in Paris (see box on page 16). Its market has reinvigorated the second-hand market, challenged traditional retail models and connected collectors from all over the world.

EBay has also fulfilled some of the overblown predictions

The History of Auctions and Flea Markets

500BC	Wife auctions held in Ancient Greece
AD193	Entire Roman Empire auctioned off
7th century	Possessions of deceased Buddhist monks auctioned in China
1595	First recorded use of the word auction, according to the *Oxford English Dictionary*
1679	London Tea Auction held
17th century	Auctions held in British taverns and coffeehouses to sell art
1744	Sotheby's was founded
1766	Christie's was founded
1832	Cholera epidemic prohibited markets in the centre of Paris
1880	Poor of Paris made their living selling rags, metal and food
1887	Fruit and vegetables were sold in Dutch auctions
1920	First organized market was opened in Paris; beginnings of Le Marché aux Puces
September 1995	AuctionWeb (to be known as eBay) launched
1996	William Vickery wins Nobel Prize for pioneering work on economics of auctions

made during the dotcom boom of the late 90s. When the internet exploded onto the world's consciousness, many promises were made. We were told that technology could facilitate access to a global village by providing users with genuine connections between one another.

While a ream of ambitious dotcom businesses held champagne parties, talked about a revolution and effortlessly burned through millions of dollars of venture capitalist funding, eBay quietly built a global marketplace to connect individuals. With an eye on an old-fashioned era, eBay rejuvenated the concept of more personal customer service.

While a European start-up called boo.com burned through £80m ($150m) launching a website that sold designer clothes through an avatar called Ms Boo, eBay nurtured a self-regulating community and developed a set of tools so traders need never leave the confines of the site, all on a global scale.

In January 2000, 17 dotcom companies paid over $2m each for a 30 second TV spot at the US Superbowl. These companies had been dictated by the rules of the new economy, which said that a customer base must be grown at all costs, even if it led to massive losses.

Just four months later, on April 14 2000 when the dotcom bubble burst, it was the end of a weird and wonderful rollercoaster ride for many opportunist start-ups. Every day, journalists and analysts began to check the new tombstones in the dotcom graveyard on a website called fuckedcompany.com.

While the Nasdaq dived by 355 points and the Dow Jones fell by 617 points, both historic falls, Meg Whitman, eBay's CEO, insisted that eBay would come through, announcing strong quarterly results. "EBay is positioned to thrive, not just survive this shakeout." She was right. Many early stars like webvan, pets.com and boo.com crumbled to dust, but eBay is still standing and thriving.

AUCTION CULTURE

EBay is changing society. It is a brand for the lease economy, a brand for consumers who don't necessarily want to own possessions for ever. Dan Nissanoff, author of *Futureshop*, believes society is moving from an accumulation to an auction culture. He says it's a philosophy that recognizes temporary ownership as more effective.

There's no doubt that secondary markets are thriving on eBay. They enable consumers to access premium brands that would have previously been out-of-reach. Traders must consider the resale value of new goods. It may be worth spending an extra $300 on a designer baby's pushchair, if you can sell it again for $400 on eBay.

Meanwhile, in the lease economy, buyers are becoming empowered. It is up to them to place a price on the value of brands. They may not be able to control how much an item costs in the high-street, but eBay's perfect market, the point where supply meets demand, will value products fairly.

EBay has created a twilight world that's ruled by "time remaining," where the streets are paved with bubble wrap and the daily arrival of the postman has seminal importance. It's a parallel universe where people are called dave's loveshack, jo's big toe, pinkymoon, moneymonster and verynaughty fairy. Being part of the eBay universe is like being in love. People forget to eat; they're so busy buying stuff.

PINNING DOWN THE EBAY BUTTERFLY

For a brand with such big ambitions, eBay doesn't like to talk much. It may have changed society and revolutionized marketplaces, but it would prefer we found this out for ourselves. It prefers to keep its leadership out of the limelight and let its community do the talking.

This is a new-generation brand, one that's shaped through its rabble of noisy traders. EBay could not be neatly summarized in a brand book or PowerPoint presentation. Hence my requests to interview eBay executives were turned down. Emails direct to management were politely ignored. Discussions with eBay employees were off-the-record and discreet. Loitering outside eBay HQ in the UK was fruitless.

But the Greek chorus – eBay's community talked and talked. They sang me the eBay song, they emailed me essays and book proposals they'd written, they emailed and ISM'd me, they met me face-to-face, they chatted about me on the message boards. They loved eBay but sometimes they hated eBay. They needed eBay, but eBay also needed them.

I attended eBay University. I bought and sold items I didn't need, but desperately wanted until I earned my first yellow star. I lingered on eBay's chat rooms all over the world. And I talked to those on the periphery of the eBay effect, the former employees, the consultants, the businesses that fuel the phenomenon. I even auctioned chapter seven of this book.

The collection of stories that follows is an independent account of the inexorable rise of eBay. It's the tale of an eccentric global brand with flaws and kinks. A brand that struggles to be defined or pinned down, aside from its tellingly symbiotic relationship with a noisy rabble of consumers. It's the tale of a brand that valued a human soul at $504 and taught over 250 million strangers to trust one another.

Chapter 2
Pierre's PEZ

> "I like to think we're a different kind of company, because of the way we interact with our community. If we lose that, we've pretty much lost everything. If you're starting a revolution and you succeed, then are you still a revolutionary? It's a little bit weird, but I think we still have a long way to go, bringing the level playing field to the rest of the world."
>
> **Pierre Omidyar, founder of eBay[6]**

Pierre Omidyar, the founder of eBay, is an accidental billionaire. In fact, he's a reluctant billionaire. From the moment eBay made him rich he became increasingly uncomfortable and even embarrassed by his newfound riches. "Don't make it grow," he once whispered to an investment adviser.[7]

Omidyar is not a classic dotcom success story. He was a French-Iranian programmer who took a chance on a quirky little website called AuctionWeb. Unlike many other entrepreneurs of his generation, he wasn't interested in the bounty that the internet might provide, but inspired by what technology could enable people to achieve.

Today, Omidyar has morphed from his dotcom entrepreneur image into something a little different. The frizzy ponytail has been tamed into a short, spiky haircut, while the Silicon Valley programmer's uniform of shorts and flip flops has been upgraded to jeans and shirt.

In 1999, when Omidyar became the richest 32-year-old in the world, worth $4bn, he cleared out his eBay cubicle and moved to Paris, with his wife Pam. Very early on, they pledged to give away nearly all of their wealth. After several years spent in France reflecting on his newfound riches, Omidyar has returned to the US, living with his family just outside Las Vegas.

And he's dedicated the next phase of his career to philanthropy, through the Omidyar network, which will distribute over $10bn to worthy causes. EBay may have created overwhelming wealth for its founder, but it has also reinforced his philanthropic principles.

During his time leading eBay Omidyar was able to witness the curious courtship dance between strangers learning to trust one another. EBay transformed their lives: people on benefits learnt to support themselves while Guatemalan villages sold their handcrafted goods to the metropolis. "You have to ask yourself: 'Is it really true that business can only be about making money? And is it really true that if you want good things to happen in a community it has to be through a non profit?'" Omidyar questioned.[8]

THE EBAY LEGEND

Legend tells us that eBay was founded on the love of a PEZ sweet dispenser; or rather as a mechanism for Omidyar's girlfriend Pam (now wife) to trade her PEZ collection. But this isn't strictly true. Instead, its roots lie in the more prosaic tale of a laser pointer.

Omidyar had a broken laser pointer. He decided to auction it online as a way of testing his new concept. "Broken Laser Pointer," he typed into the heading. In the description he explained that the item had cost him $30 new and did not seem to work even with new batteries. He began the bidding at $1 and quickly forgot about it.

No-one bid for the broken laser pointer during its first week of auction. In the second week someone bid three dollars, then four dollars and by the end of the auction it had been sold for $14.

Omidyar contacted the winner to make sure he knew it was broken. "Sure, I enjoy fixing it up," was the swift reply. It was at this moment that Omidyar realized that eBay might just change the world.

"A TYPICAL NERD OR GEEK"

Pierre Omidyar was born in Paris in 1967. His Iranian parents met while at university in Paris. They had been sent to France from Iran in the early 1960s for a better education. Omidyar's father studied medicine while his mother studied linguistics at the Sorbonne. When Pierre was six years old they emigrated to the US, where he grew up around Washington DC.

From a very young age, Omidyar was fascinated by technology. When he was still at school he would sneak out of sports lessons to gaze at a Radio Shack TRS-80 stored in his science teacher's cabinet. He used it to teach himself to program. "I was your typical nerd or geek in high school. I forget which is the good one," he has revealed.[9]

By the time he'd reached secondary school, Omidyar was able to make money from his passion and in his first job was paid $6 an hour to computerize his school's library catalogue. It's no surprise that Omidyar, a self-confessed geek, decided to specialize in computer sciences at university. By now, he preferred to shun the PC-filled rooms at his Boston University for the trusty Mac in his bedroom.

He wanted to work as a Mac programmer and successfully applied for work experience at a Silicon Valley-based company called Innovative Data Design. After finishing his degree at the University of California, Berkeley, Omidyar worked for the Apple subsidiary Claris.

In 1991, Omidyar decided to leap out alone with a group of friends launching a start-up called Ink Development Corporation. It was founded on the premise that computer users would prefer to use a pen for communicating and would abandon their keyboards. "It was going to be great; it was going to bring computers down to the rest of us. Of course, the market didn't think so," he says.[10]

Eighteen months into changing the world with a computer pen, it became clear that the revolution might not be happening after all. However, Ink Development had also been developing other e-commerce tools, which seemed to be faring better. The fledgling company relaunched as eShop, an electronic retailing company. Omidyar left because he wanted a job that would let him "do internet things."[11] He retained a sizeable stake and two years later, when Microsoft acquired eShop, he became a millionaire. And he wasn't even 30 yet.

His next job was at General Magic, a start-up founded by ex-Apple employees building computers that could speak to telephones and fax machines. It was here that he began to dabble with the idea of a perfect marketplace; here, the idea of eBay took root.

THE PERFECT MARKET

Pierre Omidyar had a vision of democracy. He believed that the Internet could create a perfect market. A place where individuals could connect with other individuals. A place where they could trade goods with one another, without being diverted into a centralized source. "This is something I really believe can be a fundamentally good human thing," he told one VC afterwards.

It would be an environment where everyone was on an equal footing and the marketplace set the price. He said: "I had a strong feeling of let's give the power to individuals. I wanted to create a level playing field where individuals could compete with big companies."[12] He wanted to nurture the financial and personal empowerment when a person has access to an efficient market.

Omidyar was not a particular fan of auctions. But he did think that they were a good market mechanism for reaching the right value of an item. Previously, the concept of a perfect market had only existed in economic theory. Omidyar believed that the auction format would be able to achieve the perfect price, just as economic theory said it should, because items would be able to sell at the point where supply met demand.

Buyers would have exactly the same information about products as each other, and sellers would all be selling their wares from the same starting line, whether they were one individual or a large corporation.

EBay began its life determined to level the playing field for small businesses and individuals. In pursuing its ambition, it has, though, grown into a large corporation itself. It's a paradox that isn't lost on its idealistic founder:

"I like to think we're a different kind of company, because of the way we interact with our community. If we lose that, we've pretty much lost everything. If you're starting a revolution and you succeed, then are you still a revolutionary? It's a little bit weird, but I think we still have a long way to go, bringing the level playing field to the rest of the world."[13]

AUCTIONWEB AND THE EBOLA VIRUS

In its early chaotic days, eBay was called AuctionWeb and squashed onto Omidyar's muddled, personal home page. AuctionWeb had to fight for attention among three other websites. Two represented companies that Omidyar's fiancée Pam was working for, while one belonged to Omidyar. It was an information source on the Ebola virus. It included a photograph of the virus and links to news stories about Ebola outbreaks.

It was 1995 and Omidyar was working at General Magic and in his spare time writing the software that would become eBay. It took him just one weekend in September to build the site. At that time his odd mix of internet sites was located on a homepage called

Echo Bay Technology Group. When he'd decided to register the name, echobay.com was taken so he settled for an abbreviation: ebay.com. "Turned out to be a lucky choice," he recalls.[14] Omidyar continued to use AuctionWeb as a brand name until 1997.

The site was not much to look at. It had just seven categories: computer hardware and software, consumer electronics, antiques and collectibles, books and comics, automotive and miscellaneous. Everything was set against a dull, grey background and the site looked like the clunky newsgroups that dominated the early internet. Omidyar's simple computer code enabled AuctionWeb users to do just three things: list items, view items and bid for items.

A few months after its launch, AuctionWeb was listing 18 items for auction unrelated to computers. It was an eclectic, eccentric mix and included gold membership to a health club for $400, a 1967 Superman lunch box for $22 and an autographed photo of Elizabeth Taylor for $200. Just one week later, the list had grown to 30 items and included a 35,000 sq ft warehouse in Idaho, where the bidding started at $325,000.

One of the first items to be listed on the site most vividly remembered by Omidyar was a 1939 silver Rolls-Royce. Omidyar thinks one of the reasons it sticks so clearly in his mind is because the listing included scanned photographs of the luxurious car. It didn't sell. Nonetheless, in 1996, after its first full year of trading, AuctionWeb had generated sales of around $6m.

AUCTIONWEB'S TEAM

By the end of 1995, AuctionWeb had grown to host 10,000 individual bids. The service was still free because Omidyar continued to run the site in his spare time from home. However, his internet hosting company began to complain that AuctionWeb traffic was slowing down its servers and they started to charge $250 a month.

This changed everything. It meant that Omidyar had to charge AuctionWeb's users if he didn't want to be out of pocket himself. He decided to charge sellers a small fee based on a percentage of their final auction price. He would charge five percent for items sold under $25 and 2.5 percent for those above.

It was a risky move and could have spelled the end of the nascent auction house. Fortunately, envelopes began to trickle through Omidyar's post box. They were stuffed with crumpled dollar notes, written cheques and some included cards with coins stuck onto them. At the end of the first month of his new strategy, Omidyar totalled the jumble of payments and realized he was making a small profit.

Before long, a flock of money-filled envelopes was falling through Omidyar's letter box. In March 2006, he collected $1,000, in April $2,500, and in May $5,000. The envelopes were piling up so fast that Omidyar didn't have time to open them; he employed the brother-in-law of a friend to take the money to the bank. In June, revenues doubled again to $10,000. AuctionWeb had become a real business and it was time for Omidyar to leave General Magic. "I had a hobby that was making me more money than my day job," he says.[15]

But even when he left General Magic there was no respite for Omidyar. He was working all hours on AuctionWeb, rewriting code, replying to emails and keeping it running smoothly. He realized it was time to hire a business partner who would help formulate a proper business strategy before he got buried in piles of envelopes and unanswered emails.

Jeff Skoll and Omidyar had met through friends. Skoll had just completed an MBA at Stanford and was working for Knight-Ridder Information, a large newspaper firm, formulating their internet strategy. Omidyar had approached Skoll to join AuctionWeb when it was just a few months old, but Skoll had not been impressed.

"I told Jeff there were people buying and selling on the

internet who never see each other but actually send money back and forth. He said, 'that's ridiculous.'"[16] However, Skoll was becoming more intrigued by the online auction and agreed to do some consulting work. Six months later, in August 1996, he joined full-time.

Skoll was a Jewish Canadian who grew up in Quebec. An entrepreneur from an early age, he studied his first degree in electrical engineering at the University of Toronto before founding two high-tech companies of his own. Skoll and Omidyar were well-suited as business partners, they've been described as yin and yang – the perfect balance.

When Omidyar recalls hiring his business partner, he talks about how he purposefully sought to employ someone who was smarter than he was, with business expertise. Although Omidyar had the experience of launching a start-up, he's always said he comes from a technical background, rather than a business one.

Initially, Skoll focused on two priorities: finding office space and making AuctionWeb look more professional. Offices in Silicon Valley were a high-priced commodity in the late 1990s, so AuctionWeb made Campbell, a more suburban area, its home.

Second, after much debate, Skoll managed to persuade a reluctant Omidyar that the three other businesses on his home page were distracting and needed to go. Omidyar really didn't want to let his Ebola virus page go. He pointed out that the Ebola site had been awarded four stars by a search engine, while AuctionWeb had only been awarded three. Skoll was determined though, and finally the information page detailing a deadly, infectious virus was removed from eBay.com.

AuctionWeb was ready for its next full-time employee and Skoll approached a 27-year-old Korean-American called Mary Lou Song. She had a Master's in communications from Stanford. On first impressions, Song was a little dismayed by AuctionWeb's shabby patchwork offices, with its meeting room furnished with a folding table and two deckchairs.

But she was impressed by Omidyar and Skoll. She liked Omidyar's visionary idealism and the fact he talked about bringing people together, rather than business models or cash flows. Despite her initial concern about the state of the office, she joined AuctionWeb shortly afterwards, with the title of public relations manager. Her job description was slightly different, though: Skoll and Omidyar didn't want any publicity.

Song immediately noticed how Omidyar's idealism affected everything he did for the company, from replying to emails to setting up rules for the feedback forum. "He saw things in a really digging-deep-down-into-your-soul kind of way. Like, what are we doing with human nature here?"[17] In October 1996, the month Song joined the fledgling start-up, AuctionWeb hosted 28,000 auctions.

A COMMUNITY OF TRADERS

> ❏ We believe people are basically good.
> ❏ We believe everyone has something to contribute.
> ❏ We believe that an honest, open environment can bring out the best in people.
> ❏ We recognize and respect everyone as a unique individual.
> ❏ We encourage you to treat others the way you want to be treated.[18]

While Omidyar built a business team, a community of traders slowly formed on the website. From the very beginning, he actively included the community in AuctionWeb's strategy. He swiftly realized that: "The brand experience was defined by how one customer treats the other customer."[19] So, he set about persuading his fledgling auction community to treat each other with respect, and treat one another in the way they'd like to be treated themselves.

Omidyar recalls getting angry emails from sellers convinced they'd been ripped off. He always told them to give each other the benefit of the doubt. "I would say, 'Put yourself in the other person's shoes, maybe they don't turn on their computer every day. Don't jump to negative conclusions, maybe there's a reasonable explanation."[20] In almost every instance, Omidyar would receive an email letting him know that everything was OK after all.

His compulsion to involve the community was also driven by necessity. He needed as much help as he could get. "Members were saying, 'Gee how do we know these other people are good? We need a way to get to know people."[21] After being bombarded by emails from disputing buyers and sellers, Omidyar set up the Feedback Forum as an official channel for rating buyers and sellers, to build trust in the marketplace.

Jim Griffith, who was one of the first five employees to join eBay and is now grandly titled, the Dean of Education, remembers Omidyar's fervent belief that people were genuinely good. The whole idea of sending money off into the netherworld and expecting someone to send goods in return is a leap of faith for many. But Omidyar knew it would work.

Around the same time as the Feedback Forum Omidyar also launched the Bulletin Board, which was designed to place more of AuctionWeb's administration into the hands of its community. Instead of bombarding emailed questions to Omidyar, users could ask each other for advice and gather and share information.

The community's active involvement in the development of AuctionWeb made its members a loyal bunch. They were able to email Omidyar to suggest ideas. And miraculously, unlike many other heads of corporations, he listened. Not only that; he often implemented their ideas. In the early days, he would rewrite software and make the changes on the site every evening, based on their feedback.

It gave the eBay community a sense of ownership. And its feedback also helped to evolve the business. Omidyar readily admits that he didn't have a big plan for how the business would develop. This was where his fledgling community stepped in and helped out. They told him what to do. They told him what they wanted.

"It was letting the users take responsibility for building the community – even the building of the website. The best ideas came from the community. They are the ones that are out there actually using the product and in some cases making their living off of it. They know more than we do, generally."[22]

A COLLECTION OF AUCTIONEERS

Collectors began to flock to eBay. While the site had initially been swamped by internet enthusiasts selling computer parts, collectors from all walks of life now began to stroll around the marketplace. Covetable items such as Beanie Babies and Star Trek memorabilia began to sell like hot cakes. By late 1996, all the fastest growing categories were collectibles such as coins, stamps or vintage toys.

AuctionWeb didn't just become a trading platform for collectors, it was also a place to gather, meet fellow enthusiasts and exchange information. Traditionally, collectors have led an isolated existence, occasionally meeting their peers at fairs or auctions. But AuctionWeb brought them together more frequently and crucially enabled them to build their collections through a few clicks of a mouse.

It sounds like an unlikely partnership, but AuctionWeb helped to fuel the Beanie Baby craze. In 1996, Beanie Baby mania scaled new heights, helped by AuctionWeb. Ty Warner, the brand's founder, was featured in the *Forbes* magazine list of the richest Americans with an estimated $4bn fortune.

Bizarrely, AuctionWeb became Beanie Babies most popular retail outlet in the US. In April 1997, there were 2,500 collectible toys listed on AuctionWeb, so it gave them their own category. The auction format was working in the seller's favour too, with Beanie Babies that had previously sold for $5 in shops fetching $33. In May 1997, AuctionWeb sold a staggering $500,000 worth of Beanie Babies, which constituted 6.6 percent of the total site's volume.[23]

In just two years, Pierre Omidyar's vision of a perfect market was gaining momentum. Collectibles and antiques were playing a crucial role in accelerating AuctionWeb's growth. In 1997, computer items, which had previously dominated the site's auctions, made just 14 percent of listings. Antique collectibles had mushroomed to make nearly 80 percent.[24] Collectors were carrying eBay away from its humble broken-laser-pointer beginnings.

Chapter 3

The Great eBay Flood

> "The past is another country, they do things differently there."
> *The Go-Between*, LP Hartley

1997 is a year etched into the memories of the early eBay employees. It was the year that eBay almost spun out of control it was growing so fast. Its registered users had mushroomed from 41,000 in 1996 to 341,000. It was listing 4.3 million items, compared with 289,000 in 1996.

1997 was the year that the online auction site outgrew its experiment and evolved into a real company. It officially swapped its birth name AuctionWeb for the more mature-sounding eBay. It received venture funding and begun to search for a long-term chief executive. It was an important year.

The first few months acquired a nickname: The Great eBay Flood. This was because there was such heavy traffic on the online auction site. In January 1997, the site hosted 200,000 auctions, compared with 250,000 in the whole of 1996.

EBay's technology, stitched together piece by piece by Omidyar, was straining at the seams. It couldn't cope with the volume of traffic and desperately needed to be upgraded. The site kept on crashing, and some auctions were taking as long as 24 hours to upload.

The situation was desperate. Omidyar and Skoll had no choice but to actively discourage auctioneers from using the site. It was an impossible task. "It was like holding back a hurricane," Mary Lou Song has said.[25] First, eBay attempted to impose a credit approval process to siphon off sellers without strong payment records. The community was in uproar and bombarded eBay's skeleton staff with irate emails.

So Omidyar and Skoll tried to limit the number of listings a seller could make daily. First, they said that sellers with a rating of less than 100 in the feedback system could list no more than four items a day. Again, the community rebelled, saying the policy was unfair to new users. Then they tried to limit the number of items listed on the site daily. This time, the auctioneers from the West Coast of America protested loudly, complaining that their East Coast competitors were getting the lion's share of listings because they woke three hours earlier.

Finally, the management team imposed time limits. AuctionWeb would only accept listings during 10 minutes in every hour. As soon as the 10-minute window opened, sellers would leap into action, listing as many items as they could. This meant that they had 50 minutes an hour when they could loiter and chat on the community boards instead.

FROM AUCTIONWEB TO EBAY

On September 1 1997, the new, more robust technology platform was launched, and eBay employees attempted to cajole and persuade users to enrol manually onto the new system. It wasn't easy, eBay couldn't transfer them automatically. There were 200,000 registered users to transfer and they were reluctant to move onto a new site with fewer buyers. Even dangling the carrot of free listings did little to tempt them.

Once more, eBay employees discovered how easy it was to fuel the wrath of members of the community, if they felt they hadn't been consulted on changes. The new site also led to an expansion of auction categories, from 40 to 100. Mary Lou Song developed a comprehensive new list and posted it for the community's feedback and was again astonished by both the vehemence of feeling and level of detail among the community's responses.

Button collectors were especially angry at being ignored by eBay. "Did you know that buttons don't belong in sewing collectibles? That they belong in their own button category," ranted one irate button seller. Song meekly collaborated with the community and revised the listings.[26]

The new technology platform also provided an opportunity for AuctionWeb to officially rebrand itself as eBay. While the domain name had always been eBay.com, the site had been called AuctionWeb, which was confusing. Moreover, eBay didn't even own the domain name for AuctionWeb.com.

A SUITABLE MARRIAGE

1997 was also the year when Skoll managed to sketch out eBay's first business plan. In a section called "philosophy," Skoll loftily imagined how the internet might resuscitate old-fashioned relationships between buyers and sellers. Internet auctions represent, "the opportunity for mankind to recapture the lost ambiance of the town market, when personal interaction and personal attention was the key to a trade and to life in general," he wrote.[27]

What's fascinating about the first business plan is Omidyar and Skoll's pessimism about eBay's prospects. They believed that established internet players such as AOL or Yahoo would launch their own online auctions and dwarf their own start-up. They thought their future lay in licensing online auctioning technology to other businesses. The business plan concluded: "EBay sees AuctionWeb as a 12–18 month gambit, after which eBay will consider selling the service or paring back the investment."[28]

With business plan in hand, Omidyar and Skoll decided to look for strategic partners in mid-1997. Unlike many other dotcom start-ups, they were in the fortunate position of not needing cash. They were already profitable, but what they wanted, and needed, was a partner to help expand the business. They made a short list of investors they would like to talk to and met up with all of them.

The eBay entrepreneurs had already been approached by American media company, Times Mirror, which owned the *Los*

Angeles Times newspaper. At the time, Skoll and Omidyar would have been open to a deal that bought eBay for $40m. But the senior, traditional media executives got cold feet. They didn't think strangers would ever trust each other on a big scale. They also didn't understand how eBay could be worth as much as $40m when it didn't own any buildings or products.

One well-known investor who could have made a good strategic partner messed it up at the end of the meeting. He said he wouldn't value eBay at more than a certain figure, which Skoll and Omidyar had cautiously estimated was half their value. Instead, they opted for Benchmark Capital, a Californian venture capital firm, which bought 22.5 percent in the company for $5m. Unlike many of its peers, eBay put the money into a bank account, and never touched it.

There have been some critics of the eBay/Benchmark Capital deal. In hindsight, it's tempting to suggest that Benchmark struck gold. EBay didn't need funds from a venture capitalist: was a quarter of equity in the company too high a price for some strategic advice and contacts? At eBay's peak on the stock market, Benchmark Capital's stake grew in value to over $4bn, making it one of the most profitable investments a venture capitalist (VC) had ever made.

Years later, Omidyar admitted that the Benchmark Capital stake was worth "lots." But, he's adamant that he doesn't regret selling one quarter of the company for just $5m. He believes that the value the VC firm added through the flotation and in subsequent years was enormous. After all, it was Benchmark Capital that helped persuade Meg Whitman to uproot her family and join the fledgling start-up.

PRIMARY COLOURS

Another valuable piece of advice Benchmark Capital passed on to its young auctioneer was the need to redesign the home page.

While the new eBay site was in colour, a stark contrast to the monochrome greys of AuctionWeb, it was still ugly.

The brand name eBay was written in simple block letters and the home page was punctuated with two stark but random logos. First, a steaming cup of coffee, to signify the community chatroom, eBay Café, and second, an open book, which was supposed to illustrate the listing of an item.

It was an improvement on the plain black and white logo for AuctionWeb, which eBay staff nicknamed the "death bar," but it was still work in progress. Some employees were convinced the unsightly home page was scaring away potential strategic partners.

What eBay needed was a new logo. Benchmark Capital introduced eBay's management to branding expert Bill Cleary of CKS Interactive. He conducted some consumer research to see how the brand was regarded among its community. It was all good news: its users clearly understood that eBay was an online trading platform, thanks to the historical focus of the organization. However, the web auctioneer still needed a new logo.

Cleary drew six different alternatives. And one of them is the eBay logo we know and love today: e – b – a – Y written in bold, primary colours. One prototype of the logo placed eBay's B as a capital letter, reflecting how it's written in text. However, the capital B in the middle of the logo felt too much like a full stop in the middle of the brand, so the Y was capitalized instead. The colourful logo is supposed to reflect the quirky personality of the brand. The letters overlap a little to reflect the trust binding the community. As its designer explained, "it had a little bit of the ponytail about it."[29]

STORYTELLING

After two years of determined silence, eBay was ready to talk. Omidyar purposefully avoided PR and advertising for the first two years of his start-up's life. He wanted to concentrate on building the user experience first. He still firmly believes that raw hype is not a good thing.

He says the best businesses develop a good product first that generates a favourable experience for their users. When offering advice to ambitious entrepreneurs clamouring around him for words of wisdom, Omidyar warns them that hype is a bad thing. Instead, they should focus on the product experience and let the word trickle out.

Omidyar's wisdom seems obvious in hindsight, but during the heady days of the dotcom boom, most excitable entrepreneurs were blowing their venture capital funds on costly, glossy TV campaigns and extravagant launch parties.

Omidyar dressed himself up into a suit and started talking to reporters and analysts across America. His reception was quite cool. Nobody really understood what eBay was. And they certainly couldn't fathom how so many strangers could trust one another across cyber space. Some journalists cancelled their meetings with Omidyar, others couldn't promise they'd be writing anything soon.

In the late 1990s, American journalists were being bombarded with stories of start-ups and new internet ventures. There was nothing in the eBay story that grabbed their attention. Then Mary Lou Song talked to her friend Pam Wesley, Omidyar's fiancée, and discovered Pam's interest in trading PEZ dispensers online.

The eBay legend was hatched. That night Mary Lou Song called a local newspaper journalist and told him that the real inspiration for eBay's business model was to create a platform to help Omidyar's fiancée trade PEZ dispensers online. The next day, the story appeared in the local paper, the first of thousands of stories about the PEZ dispenser. The myth was born. As Song quickly realized, "Nobody wants to hear about the tale of a 30-year-old genius who wanted to create a perfect market. They want to hear that he did it for his fiancée."[30]

THE END OF AN ERA

1997 also signified the end of an era for eBay. The baby auctioneer had taken its first steps and was beginning to grow up. Days in the eBay office often ground to a halt at 3pm for a company game of football; meetings took place in a room affectionately called "The Beach," populated with deck chairs; on quiet afternoons, the entire workforce would migrate to the local cinema to watch a film.

In the summer of 1997, Omidyar and Skoll hired a vice president for marketing and business development called Steve Westly. He brought a team with him: Richard Rock and Tom Adams. The three became known as the "Three Stanford MBAs" among eBay's established workforce. They were different from the people who already worked there. They wore suits, they liked spreadsheets and PowerPoint, and they understood the importance of cash flows.

Richard Rock remembers how scary it was to join this small company called eBay that no-one had heard of. But, armed with his Stanford MBA, he was impressed by the fledgling site. He liked the fact that it had no banner ads, yet made $400,000 every month through fees. Unlike many other start-ups of the time, eBay was profitable. And on the day they joined, they built their own desks and carved themselves a space in the crowded and cramped offices.

Rock and his MBA peers felt different from their new colleagues. "Most of the employees were there for the community. It was like a hobby; they loved what they were doing. They would roll in at 10:30 in the morning in shorts and T-shirts, but our vision was that this company could be really big," elaborates Rock.

"We took a methodical approach to the business that had been like a hobby before. There was a clash of cultures. Those who had been involved in eBay in the early days were excited about its potential but they didn't want to give up anything warm and fuzzy. We represented a bit of a threat."

Rock candidly admits that there were some arguments as the two cultures fenced around each other. But there were also some valuable compromises made. In time, the old-school eBayers appreciated that it was time for the auction site to grow up; and in turn, Richard Rock and his MBA colleagues learnt to respect the importance of the community.

"It's very likely they found us overly commercial but Jeff and Pierre needed a vision of how to make eBay work. We became more considerate of the community and how deals might affect them and they became more aware of the skills we brought to help eBay," adds Rock.

The fact that eBay was growing virally all by itself meant that its development was different from that of other dotcoms. EBay didn't need to strike deals to grow; it was already doing that all by itself. This meant Rock could take a more disciplined approach and only consider deals that would add to eBay's bottom line profits. While the big internet players of the time like Yahoo and AOL were sniffing around the online auction site, they weren't used to the sort of deals eBay was proposing.

"They didn't like doing deals with us because we didn't pay as much as other internet sites. The negotiations were much harder. AOL was used to walking into a room and setting a price," recalls Rock. After much to-ing and fro-ing eBay agreed to pay AOL $750,000 in a six-month advertising deal that would drive more traffic to the online auctioneer.

There was a heated debate within eBay before the deal went ahead. The old school believed that eBay should continue to grow virally and not sell out to big corporations. They were concerned that corporate deals like the AOL one could taint the grassroots of the community and make it overly commercial.

EBay's business development team fought hard to protect the deal – they argued that eBay's viral growth couldn't last for ever, that eventually its following of collectors would dry up. Then they pointed out that the deal might prevent AOL from getting into auctions itself, something the senior management was especially concerned about. The agreement was signed.

Rock is proud of the four years he spent at eBay. He's particularly proud of the fact that in the early days the business development team refused to sign any deals that wouldn't generate profit for the online auction site. He says he decided to leave because he was tired; he'd made some money from the eBay flotation and he wanted to travel.

On the day he left the company, as he was sending a goodbye email to his colleagues, he returned to a set of goals that had been written when he'd joined. One was to be the biggest company on the internet. The day he left, eBay's market capitalization exceeded Yahoo's for the first time.

In four short years, the little internet company with 100,000 items for sale, which had interviewed him on a deckchair and asked him to build his own desk, had grown to become a global brand. "It's rewarding to know I've been part of something as fundamental as eBay," he says, proudly.

PREPARING FOR WAR

But let's rewind again to 1997, when eBay still had a lot of growing to do before it would overtake Yahoo and become a global brand.

At the start of the year, it had still not faced serious competition. This was to change in October, when two well-funded auction sites Auction Universe and Onsale Exchange muscled into eBay's arena. Onsale had been on the scene for a while, but it had a subtly different business model from eBay. Rather than work in person-to-person auctions, it took possession of goods and auctioned them off itself. Realizing it should change, Onsale asked eBay to sell its registered email addresses. EBay refused, but its technology department soon noticed bots roaming its website trying to collect email addresses.

It wasn't long before Onsale Exchange, a person-to-person auction, was launched. Many of eBay's users were emailed and invited to try the new site for free. Messages appeared in eBay's chat rooms promoting the new auction service.

It is said that eBay prepared for war, quite literally, at this point. Key employees were given military helmets and dog tags and the walls were encased with army camouflage. Jeff Skoll set up two computers, one to monitor Onsale Exchange and the other to monitor Auction Universe.[31]

Auction Universe was the number two auction site, after eBay and it had recently been acquired by the media group Times Mirror, who had initially courted eBay. It only had around 1,000 auctions running at any one time, but it was banking on drawing on its media heritage by pulling in more users with editorial content.

By the summer of 1997, Auction Universe was hosting around 15,000 auctions and was causing alarm at eBay HQ. Then, inexplicably, Auction Universe's meteoric growth began to level off. It would seem that eBay's home-grown charm was more appealing to auctioneers than the slick corporate façade of Auction Universe.

More importantly, eBay's sellers and buyers were loyal to the site because of its feedback system. They had built themselves a valuable online reputation, and they didn't want to walk away from it. They were also loyal to each other and didn't want to leave the eBay community behind them. As Mary Lou Song noted: "It's not so much that our users were that loyal to eBay; eBay was part of the equation, but they were really loyal to each other."[32]

First-mover advantage doesn't always work in a business's favour but it did for eBay. Omidyar and Skoll believed it was because their business created a "virtuous circle." Sellers came to eBay because that's where all the buyers were; buyers came to eBay because that's where the sellers were. EBay was not a traditional e-commerce site but a virtual network, and that's why building a critical mass of users was so important.

The same idea is explained by an internet phenomenon called the network effect. One consequence of it is that the purchase of something by one individual indirectly benefits others who own the goods – for example, by buying a telephone a person makes other telephones more useful.

The network effect was often cited during the dotcom boom of the late 1990s to overemphasize the importance of market share over profit among young, growing companies. It was certainly relevant to some business models. A good example is Mirabilis, the Israeli start-up that pioneered instant messaging and was bought by AOL. Mirabilis purposefully gave away its product for free to corner the market.

The network effect is also relevant in eBay's case. The value of its marketplace to a new user is proportional to the number of other users in the market. As the number of eBay users grows, the auctions become more competitive and the bids get higher. This brings more sellers onto the site.

The arrival of more sellers drives prices down again because it increases supply, while bringing more people onto the site. Essentially, as the number of users of eBay grows, prices fall and supply increases, and more people find the site useful. (Skype, the voice over internet telephony service, which eBay acquired in 2005, is another business model that thrives from the network effect.)

While both Onsale Exchange and Auction Universe continued to plod along, they failed to threaten eBay to the same extent again. Auction Universe was renamed auctions.com and sold to another traditional media company. Onsale's management suggested a merger, but eBay decided to carry on alone and upgrade its servers instead.

COMING OF AGE

At the end of 1997, eBay had survived and thrived during a critical year. It had fought off competition, signed a major deal with AOL, relaunched its site, shared a PEZ legend with the press, painted itself in colour and secured funding. Some of its community had left and come back again and it had mushroomed in size. An eBay fanatic had invented the first wave of sniping software that enabled an auction to be won right at the last minute. Life at eBay would never be the same again.

EBay's coming of age was confirmed when Omidyar decided it was time to replace the deckchairs and self-assembly desks. He drove to Apple's offices, which had a surplus of furniture, and bought a job-lot of cubicles for eBay's 50 staff. Immediately, the start-up atmosphere in eBay's offices was dampened. There were no more office football games, as the playing field was filled with cubicles.

The point of no return probably came when Omidyar and Skoll hired a chief financial officer, Gary Bengier. Like the new business development team, he was a grown-up employee with a Harvard MBA and 20 years' experience of finance. Symbolically, Bengier's desk was assembled for him; he didn't have to build it himself.

There was just one final piece in the transition jigsaw to be filled: a chief executive. During the autumn of 1997, Omidyar and Skoll began interviews. There was one favoured candidate, a woman called Margaret Whitman. But eBay's investors Benchmark Capital, who had made the introduction and said she would be perfect, feared they'd never be able to persuade her to join the company.

Chapter 4

Mystic Meg

> "Ask anyone about me, and they would never think of power. You know, you say 'sky,' and they say 'blue.' Say 'power' and no-one would say Meg Whitman."[33]
>
> **Meg Whitman**

A middle-aged woman, with a shy smile, strolls onto a vast stage that dwarfs her tall frame. She's dressed casually in beige, belted trousers and a pale blue polo shirt, with an eBay logo. Her blonde, bobbed hair skims below her chin. She giggles nervously as over 15,000 of her customers chant her name: "Meg! Meg! Meg! Meg!"

The woman is about to address the crowd at eBay Live!, the networking event for online auctioneers, who enjoy the annual opportunity to meet their eBay friends face-to-face. In 2006, the fifth eBay Live! was held in Las Vegas in late June and sold out for the first time. It had attracted a crowd of over 15,000 eBayers, who visited the show from more than 35 countries.

The whistles and cheers fade as she prepares to speak to the ocean of faces gazing at her. "Well, welcome to Las Vegas!" exclaims Meg Whitman, the president and CEO of eBay. "It's such a thrill to see you at the biggest eBay Live! ever!" The crowd responds with more excitable whoops and cheers. As her speech comes to an end, they are showered with eBay-coloured confetti and balloons, while Elvis sings, "Viva Las Vegas!"

During the rest of the event, Whitman spends her time playing the role of Meg as celebrity. She works the crowds, signing T-shirts and trading cards that feature pictures of her fly-fishing (a hobby.) Each eBay customer is asked the same question by its president and CEO: "Where are you from? What do you sell?" They form a long snake that curls around the Vegas hotel, all desperate for the chance to meet Meg face-to-face. As she hears of each fledgling eBay business success, she congratulates them maternally, "There you go!"

The community loves the fact they might bump into Whitman during eBay Live! Andrew Dudley, a full-time eBay trader has got a picture of himself with her on his website. "She intermingles with the crowd, which is brilliant. She's down-to-earth and understands the community, which is the Holy Grail."

Just a few weeks after Las Vegas is stripped of eBay devotees, Whitman-signed copies of the eBay Live! brochures are being auctioned with bids over $10. Proud eBayers are displaying photographs of themselves shaking hands with Meg on their websites; Whitman has probably made thousands of autograph-seeking eBay fanatics very happy indeed.

AN UNDERSTATED PRESIDENT

Meg Whitman was an unlikely chief executive. She didn't quite fit the mould of a suit-wearing, MBA-brandishing, ball-breaking, limelight-grabbing leader. Jim Rose, the former president of QXL, one of eBay's most formidable competitors in Europe, describes her understated stance: "She has a personality and a style which is very maternal. She's not a yeller or a screamer, or even a hard core business person, which suits eBay's community."

But that's not to say that she wasn't highly respected by her peers, investors and analysts. In 2005, *Vanity Fair* magazine ranked her as the seventh most powerful figure in the world, ahead of US investor Warren Buffet. She's also been named the most powerful woman in business by *Fortune* magazine. AG Lafley, CEO of Procter & Gamble, is one of her great admirers. He describes her power in terms of influence: "It's not about control, and I don't think it's about size. The measure of a powerful person is that their circle of influence is greater than their circle of control."

Her admirers appreciate her soft touch, they point out that people aren't threatened by her. As one peer says: "Meg is Meg. She is who you meet. She's smart, straight, and to the point. She's just really nice to do business with." Apparently, the only time she dictates is during meetings. She likes to tell people where to sit. Whitman laughingly suggests this is because her mother always said a thoughtful seating plan was the secret to successful dinner parties.

Whitman recalls a piece of advice given to her at the age of 10 by her father. He told her to be nice to people. He said: "There's no point in being mean to anyone at any time. You never know who you're going to meet later in life. And by the way, you don't change anything by being mean. Usually you don't get anywhere."[34]

Unlike many leaders, Whitman is uncomfortable talking about her power. She likes to understate her influence and modestly point towards the customers who have built eBay. She says she doesn't actually think of herself as powerful. "Ask anyone about me, and they would never think of power. You know, you say 'sky,' and they say 'blue.' Say 'power' and no-one would say Meg Whitman."[35]

Aside from sidestepping the spotlight, Whitman was also known for her eBay uniform. She always wore the same outfit, a polo shirt and beige trousers. It's the same as other eBay employees. During one magazine interview she invented a new tongue-in-cheek tagline for herself: "She's frumpy, but she delivers."[36]

She also forfeited the conventional CEO slick executive suite with panoramic views, leather-swivel designer chair and deep pile carpet for something a little simpler: a cubicle in eBay's open plan office. It was a real cubicle with short walls and cluttered surfaces piled with paper. It's a typical environment for a Silicon Valley start-up, but not a multi-billion dollar enterprise.

HUNTING FOR A GROWN-UP

In the autumn of 1997, eBay's partners Pierre Omidyar and Jeff Skoll decided it was time to find a grown-up chief executive to lead their newly adult company. Their investors Benchmark Capital helped to start the search, putting them in touch with headhunters and putting forward some suitable names.

Skoll and Omidyar had no qualms about appointing a more experienced chief executive. They were unusually pragmatic about their strengths and weakness as leaders. They knew that they were entrepreneurs, but that as eBay grew larger and older, a different kind of management was required. "They deserved so much credit for stepping back from their baby, their idea," recalls Rock.

Both eBay and Benchmark Capital agreed that the most important quality in a new CEO was an understanding of consumer marketing and an appreciation of eBay's unique culture and community. They had to be, in Omidyar's words, "eBaysian."[37]

Some candidates immediately proved themselves to be utterly unsuitable for the position. One flew first class to the interview and pulled up outside eBay HQ in a limousine. Another, ignorant of eBay's leadership, suggested that it could be possible for eBay to emulate competitor Onsale's success.

Then there was Meg Whitman. Pierre Omidyar has recalled how her name was highlighted on the first list of 70 names drawn up by Benchmark Capital. One of the investors pointed to it, saying, "Boy, she would be great, but we could never get her." The hurdle was a big one: Whitman wasn't interested in the job.

When Whitman was first called about the eBay job, she declined to attend the interview. She didn't want to uproot her family 3,000 miles to the West Coast of America and was enjoying working in a senior marketing position at Hasbro, the toy company. Her husband had become head of neurosurgery at

Massachusetts General Hospital and her two sons were settled in school. Life was good.

Then Benchmark called again and tried to persuade Whitman to meet Omidyar and Skoll. Reluctant to alienate an influential Silicon Valley headhunter, she agreed to fly to California. The night before, Whitman gazed at the eBay website to prepare herself for the interview. She was not impressed.

Whitman spent the whole day in California with Omidyar, Skoll and Bob Kagle from Benchmark Capital. And by the end of their meeting it dawned on her what a big opportunity eBay could become. "I saw that Pierre had created an entirely new market. This was the creation of something that couldn't be done offline. The second thing that struck me was the emotional connection between eBay users and the site. It was clear to me that eBay had the makings of a really great brand."[38]

Whitman was impressed by Omidyar and Skoll. She liked them and valued their good intuition. And the eBay management were impressed by her – even more in person than they had been on paper. They liked the fact that she seemed down-to-earth. And they were especially impressed by one question she asked during the interviewing process: "Pierre's not going anywhere is he?"

From this insightful comment, Kagle was convinced that they'd found the right person for the job. "It's relatively rare that you find a new CEO mature enough to be more concerned about keeping the good people than making their mark and taking control. Her comment displayed an unusual perceptiveness into the fact that what was going on at eBay was pretty special and that Pierre had been the architect of it," he says.[39]

Whitman was surprised to discover how intrigued she was by the role at eBay. She called to say she'd be interesting in returning, if they'd have her, to delve into the business and meet some more staff. She returned the day before Thanksgiving, surprisingly calm and focused considering that 40 guests would be turning up at her house in Boston the following day.

When Whitman arrived at eBay from her flight she was relieved to see a receptionist sitting at a desk to meet her. What she didn't realize was that the receptionist had been purposefully recruited to give potential CEOs a better impression of the company as they arrived for interviews. Whitman reviewed eBay's financial records and was astonished by its 30 percent monthly growth. She was also amazed by eBay's 85 percent gross margins. Omidyar, in turn, was amazed by Whitman's ability to decipher complex financial information. He remembers asking himself, "What are gross margins?"[40]

Whitman was sold. All she had to do now was convince her husband and 10-year-old and 13-year-old sons to move 3,000 miles across America. They were all happy and settled in Boston.

Whitman and her husband both liked north California and decided that it would be good for their sons to be so close to technology. The only hitch was finding another job for her husband. But then the stars aligned. As luck would have it, Stanford was searching for a director for its brain tumour programme. "That never happens, ever. You are always sort of sabotaging each other's career as you move across the country. So it just seemed like the right thing," says Whitman.[41]

WHITMAN'S STORY

The youngest of three children, Meg Whitman was born in August 1956 in Cold Spring Harbour, Long Island, a New York suburb. Her father worked in Wall Street and her mother was a housewife, who later discovered a love of travel. Whitman thought she wanted to be a doctor and studied physics and maths at Princeton University. After selling ads one summer for a magazine she switched to economics. By the age of 21, Whitman was studying for an MBA at Harvard Business School.

Her first job was as a brand manager at Procter & Gamble, where she displayed an inherent sense of consumer marketing. In a diary at this time, she wrote: "It's all about the customer." Her time at P&G also taught her the importance of always doing the best job possible, even if it's boring. She recalls being given this advice by her boss at P&G in 1979.

She was fresh out of Harvard with an MBA and desperate to sink her teeth into some meaty business problems. Instead, she was handed an assignment to determine how big the hole should be in a shampoo bottle – three eighths of an inch or one-eighth of an inch. She found it frustrating but it made her realize that every job given is an opportunity to prove yourself.

Whitman married Griff Harsh, a neurosurgeon, and they moved to San Francisco, where he'd been offered a neurosurgery residency. Whitman joined Bain and Co. as a management consultant. She worked there for eight years and was elected partner.

In 1989, she was offered a job too good to turn down – vice president of strategic planning at Walt Disney. Within 18 months, she had been promoted to senior vice president of marketing for the Disney Consumer Products Division, where she helped Disney's theme store move abroad, at some points spending a week a month in Japan.

In 1991, Whitman and her family moved to Boston, where her husband became director of the brain tumour programme at Massachusetts General Hospital. Whitman joined Stride Rite, the shoe company, before accepting an offer in 1995 to become president and CEO of Florists Transworld Delivery (FTD) based in Michigan and Illinois. Two years later, Whitman left FTD and returned to her family in Boston, who had not moved to Midwest with her.

Back in Boston, Whitman became general manager of Hasbro's pre-school division, which she revived and overhauled, returning it to profitability. It was in early 1998, while she was enjoying being back with her family, that Benchmark called her about the president and CEO position at eBay.

LISTENING AND LEARNING

Meg Whitman joined eBay as president and CEO in March 1998. She spent the first few weeks observing and listening to what was going on around her. She made appointments to speak individually to members of the senior team. "She came and, to her credit, she did a great job of having respect for what we'd built before," says Omidyar.

For Whitman, eBay was unlike any other company she'd worked at. It was still very much in start-up mode, and had just 35 employees. EBay culture wasn't used to pencilling in appointments in a calendar; if the employees had any ideas they would just stroll over and talk to one another. Whitman reflected that there was a lot to do to best prepare eBay for growth. She needed to develop a strategy, a brand positioning, an organizational structure and work out precisely what market eBay was serving.

Omidyar played a crucial role in ensuring Whitman's transition to CEO was as smooth and painless as possible. He was confident of Whitman's ability to lead the company and made every effort to communicate this trust to the eBay team. He made a presentation to the company that showed how eBay's growth and potential required a different kind of CEO. He reassured them that Meg understood the values of the eBay community.

Omidyar also made a point of delegating responsibility to Meg almost immediately. "After Meg joined, when people would come into my office looking for my decision on an issue, I would tell them, 'you need to talk to Meg about that.' Pretty quickly people got used to it."[42]

In turn, Whitman was determined to establish a close working relationship with Omidyar. She knew that he probably understood the community better than she ever would, and wanted him to be involved in every decision.

Whitman's learning curve steepened after just two weeks in

the job when the site crashed for eight hours, angering hundreds of thousands of eBayers whose auctions were jeopardized. EBay's technology system was being stretched to its limit and could no longer cope with the capacity of traffic and auctions it was being asked to manage. One of Whitman's first managerial decisions was to invest heavily in the technology to make eBay's system more robust.

'A CULT-LIKE FOLLOWING'

Omidyar was impressed by the way Whitman's consumer marketing experience enabled her to understand eBay's users. Skoll and Omidyar told her about one eBayer in a research group who said: "Oh, I don't use eBay that much. Just three or four times a day." Whitman was able to translate these nuggets of information into consumer insight. She told Omidyar and Skoll that these were passionate people. She could see that something special was going on.

Whitman began to apply her consumer marketing expertise to the start-up. She organized focus groups in San Francisco and Boston and was astonished by the broad range of eBay users. "We had people from all walks of life: a Harvard law student, a truck driver, stay-at-home moms, people of all ages. I remember thinking, 'This is going to be huge.'"[43]

That day Whitman called Pierre to tell him she'd never seen focus groups like it before. She had never seen such attachment to a company or product in 20 years of marketing. In a report for Morgan Stanley Dean Witter, "celebrity" dotcom analyst Mary Meeker neatly summarized eBay's community as: "eBay's passionate customer base (of the "this has changed my life" camp) reminds us of the cult-like following during the early and great days of Apple."[44]

Drawing on the segmentation approach she'd practised at P&G and Bain, Whitman analyzed and identified eBay's different consumer segments. There was a core group of heavy users, with 20 percent representing 80 percent of the volume on the site. One quarter of that 20 percent made a full-time living from trading on eBay.

These findings led to eBay developing its PowerSeller Program, which gave special benefits and privileges to heavy users. Powersellers had to sell a monthly minimum of $2,000 and have a 98 percent positive feedback rating. In return, they could use a special icon by their name and dedicated email customer support. Gold powersellers, who sold a minimum of $25,000 monthly even got a dedicated account manager and a 24-hour customer support line.

The consumer research also helped the eBay management team to create a brand positioning. It decided to focus on the idea that eBay was a personal trading community for individuals rather than big businesses, distinguishing itself from other auction sites.

Whitman loved to measure everything. Today, there is a host of different barometers that take the temperature of eBay's business daily. There's standard internet metrics such as how many people visit the site, how many register as users, how long they stay on the site, whether they buy or sell or both. Then there's specific metrics: which days are busiest; which time of day is busiest; what are eBayers discussing in the chat rooms; are they negative or positive about eBay's management ...

How many shoes sell an hour? How many cars sell in a day? How many beanie babies sell every minute? It's all measured. "If you can't measure it, you can't control it," says Whitman. "Being metrics-driven is an important part of scaling to be a very large company. In the early days you could feel it, you could touch it. Now that's more difficult, so it has to be measured."[45]

EBAY'S IPO: NOT BRAIN SURGERY

Whitman realized when she joined eBay that plans were afoot to launch the business on the stock exchange. And the IPO was scheduled for just six months after her starting date – September 1998. While the stock market soared in the first half of 1998, it dropped in mid-July.

It was not an ideal background for an IPO, but eBay was in a strong position. Unlike many other dotcom start-ups, it actually made money. Its gross profit margins were a staggering 88 percent, compared with 22 percent for Amazon. These metrics meant there was no reason for eBay to postpone its flotation despite the unsettled financial climate.

In September, bracing itself for the tough market, eBay began its 10 day road show. In that short time, Whitman made 79 presentations to 276 investors in 21 cities. Meanwhile, the Dow Jones index had its Bloody Monday and the Nasdaq, the stock exchange that eBay would be listed on, its worst day in history. As if that weren't bad enough, Yahoo announced it was going to launch auctions, following a deal with Onsale.

EBay floated on the stock exchange on September 24 1998. Investors were anxious; the float broke a 27-day lull in IPOs. It had been the longest dry spell on the stock market for 18 years.

And what a relief eBay must have been. The online auction site sold 3.5 million shares, raising a staggering $58m for the company. With shares priced at $18 each, eBay was valued at around $700m. On the first day of trading, stock increased in value to $54 per share, before closing at $48 per share, representing a market value of $1.9bn. It was a good day.

Meg Whitman spent the IPO in the Goldman Sachs offices on the Nasdaq trading floor with eBay's senior management. She was watching the ticker as the stock went public. Astonished by its success, she called her neurosurgeon husband in his operating room to share the good news. His response ensured her feet stayed firmly rooted to the ground. "And he said, 'That's nice. But Meg, remember that it's not brain surgery.'"[46]

GUARDIANS OF THE COMMUNITY

Protecting eBay's corporate culture became even more important after the IPO. EBay's way of doing things was one of the reasons the company was so successful. Its internal culture often mirrored its community. For example, all employees were empowered to make recommendations to the senior management. Omidyar was convinced that it was essential for the internal team to share the same values as the community. He wanted to make sure that everyone was empowered to be a guardian of the community, not just the senior management.

But this could have changed when eBay became public property. The employees had all been given stock options. Around 75 of them made many millions of dollars, while even the newest, junior employees had a windfall of hundreds of thousands of dollars once their stock options vested. As the value of the stock increased over the next nine months, Omidyar, Skoll and Whitman all became billionaires. (Omidyar owned around 42 percent of the company, Skoll 28 percent and Whitman 6.6 percent.)

But eBay's senior management didn't want its employees to become obsessed by the stock price of their newly floated company. Such pre-occupation with money and wealth was distinctly un-eBaysian. It wasn't in tune with a start-up that had been founded on counting pennies, building your own desk and putting the needs of the community first.

Whitman, Skoll and Omidyar warned their staff not to get caught up in the volatility of stock options. They told them that they were building the company to last, for the long term; that it was important that they didn't focus on the stock price like so many other Silicon Valley start-ups did.

It was almost impossible, though, to contain the excitement of the eBay team. Those who'd worked at eBay since the early days were not only thrilled at the prospect of wealth, they were also exhilarated by the fact that the work of the young business had been recognized. After years of working for a website that many people didn't understand, and certainly underestimated, they were now working for a highly valuable brand.

To keep a lid on IPO fervour, Whitman imposed a restriction on how frequently staff could check the stock price. They were allowed to look at it once in the morning, and once in the evening. But the employees still managed to check out their stock options sneakily when no-one was looking. In the meantime, Omidyar and Skoll tried to lead by example. Despite their new-found wealth, they continued to drive the same beat-up, old cars, and stayed living in the same houses.

Jay Fiore, who founded the business to business (B2B) side of eBay, recalls how carefully Whitman fostered the corporate culture. "She was continually reminding us that we were the stewards of a platform, it was not our brainchild. Instead, eBay was an extraordinary phenomenon that we were charged with growing, enhancing and improving," he reveals.

THE 1999 TECHNOLOGY CRISIS

The summer of 1999, or more specifically June 10 1999, is a date seared into Meg Whitman's memory. It was the day that eBay's site crashed for 22 hours, and she believes it was both the best and the worst thing that could have happened. "It humbled the company. We were on a rocket ship. And that really stopped any idea of, 'Gee, aren't we special.' Which was really good culturally."[47]

The eBay community was defiant and angry at the crash. The customer service teams and bulletin boards were flooded with messages from desperate sellers unable to auction their goods.

For many, auctions were their only income, and they had come to expect an uninterrupted service from eBay. But there were also those community members who tried to bolster the morale of the eBay team, offering to buy them donuts or bagels as they worked around the clock.

It was a tough time, but it was also Whitman's defining moment. Despite her lack of expertise, she swiftly became familiar with the site's servers and platforms and software and ensured the technology was overhauled and made more robust. Then she led each of eBay's 400 employees to call reams of users to personally apologize for the debacle.

But eBay still needed to win back the trust and loyalty of its community. And as a newly public company, it needed to regain the confidence of some disgruntled investors. On Friday June 11, the first trading day after the start of the crash, eBay's stock plunged by nine percent. The following Monday, it plummeted by another 18 percent. The 22-hour crash had wiped out over $6bn from eBay's market capitalization.

Wall Street was not impressed. They were baying for Whitman's resignation. Fortunately, she refused. Instead, she continued to personally respond to aggravated users who had contacted her by email, she posted apologies on eBay's chat rooms and, along with the rest of the eBay team, worked her way through the list of eBay auctioneers to call them and say sorry for letting them down.

The 1999 technology crash was not Meg Whitman's only crisis. During her 10-year tenure there were many others. There were acquisitions she should have made and acquisitions she shouldn't have touched; then there are those she paid too much for. There are countries she pulled out of, and countries she should have left well alone.

Whitman says eBay's costliest mistakes always happen when it doesn't listen to the community. And running eBay today is far more complex than when she joined the ambitious start-up. In

1998, becoming the CEO of eBay was like being made mayor of a small town. Today, it's the equivalent of running a large country. As Meg Whitman approached her 10th anniversary as eBay CEO in March 2008, it was no surprise to see her step down from her role. She once said that no CEO should stay longer than a decade in the same job, so she decided to follow her own advice. Her successor, John Donahoe, a former managing partner of Bain consulting firm, who joined eBay in 2005, had a tough act to follow.

Chapter 5

Perfect Strangers

"Most people are honest. However, some people are dishonest or deceptive. It's a fact of life. But here, those people can't hide. We'll drive them away. Protect others from them. This grand hope depends on your active participation. Become a registered user. Use our feedback forum. Give praise where it is due; make complaints where appropriate ... Deal with others the way you would have them deal with you. Remember that you are usually dealing with individuals, just like yourself. Subject to making mistakes. Well-meaning, but wrong on occasion. That's just human,"

Pierre Omidyar, February 26 1996[48]

AN EBAY RITUAL

A sea of bodies stands and slightly sways in a shabby hotel banquet room in Covent Garden, London. Overlooked by 10 dusty chandeliers, they shuffle and squirm in their places, a little embarrassed and wary about what lies ahead. Meanwhile, a bouncing eBay employer, decked in an eBay University-branded, black polo shirt asks people in the audience with a feedback rating of less than 50 to sit down. A handful of people, including me, lower themselves onto our gold-flecked chairs.

It continues. People with less than 100 sit down, followed by less than 500, less than 1,000, 5,000 and 10,000. Then there are just a handful of people left standing. No longer wary, they're swelling with pride, while the rest of the room cranes their necks to see who these successful eBayers might be. Most of them seem to be friends and are sitting at the back of the room, like the cool kids at school. The final man left standing has a 39,000 feedback rating. He's given an eBay umbrella, although it turns out later that he's already got three and an eBay fleece at home.

This is an eBay ritual. It happens across the world at eBay universities and eBay events where eBayers' feedback is compared and congratulated. At eBay Live! in Las Vegas in June 2006, eBay's chief executive Meg Whitman asked everyone to pat their neighbour on their back during her keynote speech. It turned out that the 15,000 people gathered in the vast space had a combined total feedback of 15 million.

"You truly are an amazing group," she yelled at the room to whoops and cheers and a flock of eBay-coloured balloons. "Every year, there's more people standing – I love this tradition." Just before eBay Live!, the 200th million eBay member registered. That means that if the community were a nation, it would be the fifth largest in the world, with only China, India, Indonesia and the US ahead.

And eBay is like a country. Not just because of its vast population, but because of the way that the community is an intrinsic part of the business model. It is a nation peopled by its community. Members like to get involved; they are involved. They provide the living, breathing, organic messiness of eBay, which is where its vibrancy, edge and appeal lie.

EBay's brand is moulded and guided by its community. EBay members worldwide have left more than three billion feedback comments for one another regarding their transactions. The members of this vast, online community trust one another, although they've rarely met. EBay has fostered the idea that trust between strangers can be established over the internet.

EBay openly acknowledges that its business model would not be a success without its community. In 2006, Douglas McCallum, the eBay chief executive in the UK, explained their importance to a conference audience: "We build it, but it is their workplace, their stockroom, their bank, their café, their post room and now their telephone service."[49]

EBay can also be their local disco or nightclub. Dave Youngs and Annie Dilks from Derbyshire, Great Britain, got married in summer 2005 after meeting at a party for eBay enthusiasts in Nottingham. It was ebay.co.uk's first wedding. They got to know one another by chatting on the site's questions and answers forum. They had an eBay-themed wedding and bought outfits and paraphernalia from the site. After the wedding, Annie told a British newspaper, "I can't thank eBay enough. Dave is the best auction I've ever won."[50]

DREAMING OF A SHOOTING STAR

Take a step back and consider the concept of eBay. The whole idea of sending money off into the netherworld and expecting someone to send you something in return is a leap of faith. Yet, eBay's founder Pierre Omidyar always believed that people were genuinely good. He astutely realized that the eBay brand experience was defined by how its customers treated one another.

EBay's feedback system is one of the greatest innovations in online auctioneering. It is a public forum where buyers and sellers rate each other on transactions. Without it, strangers would find it difficult to trust one another. It is widely regarded as the backbone of the auction house's success because it builds trust in an anonymous online environment. It means bidders can have confidence that the seller will not take their money and run, while sellers are confident that the winning bidder pays for their item.

In a founder's letter posted on the site in February 1996, introducing the concept of the Feedback Forum, Omidyar wrote: "Most people are honest. However, some people are dishonest or deceptive. It's a fact of life. But here, those people can't hide. We'll drive them away. Protect others from them. This grand hope depends on your active participation.

"Become a registered user. Use our feedback forum. Give praise where it is due; make complaints where appropriate ... Deal with others the way you would have them deal with you.

Remember that you are usually dealing with individuals, just like yourself. Subject to making mistakes. Well-meaning, but wrong on occasion. That's just human."[51]

The rules are simple. Following a transaction, users award each other a rating of plus one, minus one or neutral and include a written explanation. These can vary from "Fast payment, great eBayer, A+++" to "Buyer beware, don't use this eBayer." Users with a rating of −4 or more are expelled from the site.

EBay's software then adds up the score and places this number after a user's name on the site. A system of coloured stars – yellow, blue, turquoise, purple, red and green – also appears as shorthand, correlating to different feedback levels and culminating in shooting stars for a feedback rating over 10,000.

What the different eBay feedback stars mean

Yellow Star ☆ 10 to 49 points

Blue Star ☆ 50 to 99 points

Turquoise Star ☆ 100 to 499 points

Purple Star ☆ 500 to 999 points

Red Star ☆ 1,000 to 4,999 points

Green Star ☆ 5,000 to 9,999 points

Yellow Shooting Star ⭐ 10,000 to 24,999 points

Turquoise Shooting Star ⭐ 25,000 to 49,999 points

Purple Shooting Star ⭐ 50,000 to 99,999 points

Red Shooting Star ⭐ 100,000 or more points[52]

Aside from building trust, the feedback system ties eBayers to the online auction site. After building up a 10,000 rating, they're unlikely to move their business to a competitor. While positive feedback can build and nurture eBay businesses, negative feedback can crush ambitious entrepreneurs and drive grown men and women to tears.

Even the most experienced eBay businessmen become upset when they believe they've received undeserved, negative feedback. It's their reputation on the line. However, no-one expects perfection: 99 percent positive feedback is good enough. As one powerseller says, "There's always an occasional nutter!" News of an eBayer with a 14,000 rating and 100 percent positive feedback is greeted with awed incredulity.

Positive feedback enables traders to sell goods for more money. It buys them the goodwill of buyers if their package is delayed. However, the system is not entirely reliable. Some buyers are nervous of leaving negative feedback, in fear of retaliation.

The feedback system has always inspired high emotions. Early in its history, eBay management learnt the danger of making strategic decisions without involving its community. The creation of the coloured stars in the feedback system in the late 1990s initially caused uproar. Mary Lou Song, eBay's third full-time employee after founder Pierre Omidyar and Jeff Skoll, developed the system and posted her proposal on eBay's bulletin board for users to view.

She was shocked to discover the strength of feeling that poured from the eBay community. They were disappointed that they hadn't been consulted earlier on in the process. Song's choice of green was particularly unpopular and led to email messages along the lines of "are you insane?" She was taken aback by the extent to which the eBay community expected to be involved. As she has said: "If McDonald's unveils a new sandwich, people just decide to buy it or not. They don't say, 'Why didn't you talk to me?'"[53]

The importance of community resonates among eBay's senior management today. The community is often told: "You are eBay. You are our business. You are why we're as big as we are." As eBay's chief executive Meg Whitman explained the online auction site's latest deal with search engine Yahoo to the eBay Live! 2006 audience, she added: "We've learnt we make our best decisions by collaborating with our community. This deal with Yahoo is no different."

EBAY UNIVERSITY

Returning to the shabby hotel room in Covent Garden, London, where some eBay university delegates are visibly concerned by an acrid smell of smoke. All is well; assure the eBay staff, it's just the hotel testing broken generators. The hotel is rather grandly called the Connaught Rooms. Their faded grandeur belies a different past. Today, it's a warren of staircases, plastic potted plants, worn carpets scarred with cigarette burns and vast, high-ceilinged rooms full of trestle tables and chairs.

The delegates are split into three different streams – Back to Basics, a course for inexperienced sellers, a more advanced course and then finally the Topsellers course, for those with established eBay businesses. Everyone has different coloured name badges; the Topsellers stand proudly, while Back to Basics look at them with awe and respect.

All the world's there. EBay doesn't attract one sort of person. They're not all young, or all old, or all white, or all poor. It's a hotch potch, eclectic patchwork of society. There's a 50-year-old female black cab driver who wants to supplement her income, a Japanese boy, or is it a girl, with orange and black stripy hair, a skinhead wearing a Puma hoodie who keeps crunching Skittle sweets and a 70-year-old woman with grey hair swept into an elegant bun, who can't hear the questions.

There's a hairdresser with a manicured goatie beard, who informs the crowd he has 2,000 very special haircare products. (He already shifts 50 a week on eBay but wants to take it to the next level.) There are two tanned, blonde women dressed from head to toe in white linen – they've got 3,000 pairs of flip flops to sell. A woman in her 60s with a red face and antique gold jewellery likes to whisper to her business partner during the speeches.

One lady stands out from the crowd in the cowed Back to Basics group. Already, she's proved her eBay colours by standing for the longest during the feedback ritual to be awarded an umbrella. She is large, black and glamorous and her eBay name is misscosmopolitan. A black leather skirt is bedecked with a diamante belt, alongside gold charm bracelets, huge gold hoop earrings and a Louis Vuitton scarf. Mysteriously, she wheels a small black suitcase along with her, like an air hostess, eating cashew nuts and sipping Lucozade throughout the sessions.

During the coffee breaks, misscosmopolitan holds court. Her suitcase opens to reveal her laptop and, as the "green" eBayers cluster around her like bees to a honey pot, she shows us her eBay shop. In return, we bring her tea and biscuits. She, like many other powersellers, is generous with her knowledge. The others thirstily suck up her expertise and say they're learning more from her than the eBay university staff.

In the sessions for experienced eBayers, there's a gaggle of powersellers who sit at the back of the room. They all know each other, and whisper and heckle and giggle during introductions. They're not here to learn but to socialize and see their eBay friends. They all chat to each other regularly on the Powerseller forum and purposefully meet whenever they can at eBay events.

They're easy to spot. They wear a uniform: eBay fleece or whatever piece of eBay attire they've won, a branded T-Shirt publicizing their own eBay business and jeans. At the last event they gathered in the smoking room, but it's been taken away. So this time they're to be found smoking and gossiping on the steps of the Connaught Rooms. There are around 50 of them staying at a hotel on The Strand, just round the corner from the eBay event. They all pay for themselves and turn it into a weekend break.

In the morning, they pop down the road to Starbucks for proper coffee, while the less experienced eBayers are left with the fate of cold "coftea" – that classic conference lukewarm tipple, where hotels mistakenly top up coffee pots with tea or vice versa.

At lunchtime, these powersellers know to avoid the eBay University stale sandwich buffet. Instead, they gather at the pub across the road for some chips.

They are friends. Dotted all over the country, they talk on the phone, chat on instant messenger, email each other and gossip on the powersellers' forum. The women talk of a missing companion. She's gone dark after going for a biopsy yesterday, and they're worried about her. There's nothing unusual about this community of friends, aside from the fact that it's eBay that brought them together.

Jon, who wears an eBay fleece that he won at an event in Bristol, explains the community: "It's a social life, we talk to each other. It's like working in a pub and knowing the people who run the shop next door, so you'll borrow a cup of sugar from each other."

VIRTUAL COMMUNITIES

The word community is bandied around frequently, but what does it really mean? It is often abused as a word. Alan Mitchell, British marketing columnist, points out that it can be added to anything to give it a cosy hue.

Communities can take many forms, from tightly knit and formal to broad and informal. They can be physical or virtual. There are communities of interest, such as enthusiasts or hobbyists; communities of circumstance, such as patients, communities of status such as parents or employees. The list goes on and on.

Caroline Wiertz is a lecturer in marketing at Cass Business School in London and she specializes in virtual communities. She believes that online communities share some characteristics. The internet has given them an opportunity to interact with people with shared interests. She points out that virtual communities are more democratic than traditional communities, where people are bound together with no choice because of their location.

But why do eBayers dedicate so much of their own time to helping other buyers and sellers on the chat rooms? "To some extent it's based on the kindness of strangers," suggests Cass. "But all kindness is motivated by self interest and their contributed knowledge is visible to everyone in the community."

She believes there are two main reasons why eBayers help one another. First, is the hope of reciprocation – if you see someone stranded on the road you help them in the hope that someone will help you in a similar situation. Second, is the more selfish desire to be held in high esteem. People want to be highly regarded as experts within their community. This is another reason why eBay's feedback system works so effectively.

Cass investigated the commitment of online communities in her dissertation. She says she was continually surprised by the commitment users made to their online communities. Over 5 percent of the people she interviewed spent more than 20 hours a week in chat rooms despite the fact they had full-time jobs. One member had written a suggested etiquette on online behaviour, while another developed complex software to track the different interactions of the community.

EBay members betray similar characteristics. A number of British powersellers have founded the Federation of eBay Businesses (FOEB) to help improve eBay's reputation among non-users and are continually suggesting incremental improvements to the online auction house's business model. They attend "voice programmes" where they inform eBay's management of issues, problems and ideas to be addressed.

Cass approves of the way that eBay handles its community. "They make it clear that the real responsibility lies with the community themselves. When a business is associated with a community it's best to be hands-off. Members want the impression they're in control. It's their space, their environment; they don't want anyone to interfere too much."

SHIBBOLETH

The word shibboleth comes from the Hebrew bible. A story tells how the pronunciation of "shibboleth" was used to distinguish members of a group whose language lacked the "shhh" sound from members of a group whose dialect included the sound.

A group of people was identified and "classified" by the way they pronounced shibboleth. Today, therefore, the word has come to refer to specialist jargon within a group.

Within the eBay community, there are many smaller collectors' communities. Before eBay it was harder for these collectors both to find their desired objects and to chat to each other. It was a more isolated world; collectors might bump into each other at annual fairs or car boot sales and glean news from their community through newsletters, if they existed. But eBay has changed all that, it's made collecting more sociable.

Rebecca Ellis from Essex University has been studying the habits of eBay collectors for some time, funded by the British Economic and Social Research Council. One project has focused on Vintage Radio collectors who use their own community boards to exchange knowledge and information. One of the postings reads: "What did we do in the days BE?" [Before eBay.]

The armchair collecting potential of the internet has revolutionized their world. It means they can build their collections more quickly, but it also means that their specialist interest is no longer shrouded in mystery. Ellis analyses how some of their postings on their community board criticize eBay sellers. They enjoy deconstructing eBay descriptions that expose a seller's lack of knowledge of vintage radios.

They mock descriptions that write of "echo" rather than "ekco" or "bakerlite" rather than "bakelite." They criticize their lack of effort, their shoddy spelling and grammar and call them "idiotic sellers" and "muppets." Ellis concludes that these outpourings enable them to continue asserting their superior knowledge in their chosen field, despite the open access that eBay provides. It's an opportunity to use shibboleth.

EBayers use their community boards to find out more about buying and selling. They become a useful touchstone; the identity of bad buyers can be exposed and blocked by everyone in the chat room. They can also mock stupid buyers, sharing naïve questions with the community like: "What colour is this blue vase?"

During a focus group run by Ellis, a group of students revealed how much they used the chat rooms. "My mates do as well. They do feel part of a community and they want to look at what's going on. I'm not that bad but I do tend to want to know what's going on with eBay," said one.

But eBayers also use the community forums to chat when they're bored and to make friends. Many of them go on to meet each other in the real world, some form relationships and fall in love. They can be as close knit and compassionate as the community in a village. There was one thread on the eBay boards where an eBayer recovering in hospital from an overdose thanked the community for her get well cards.

A HISTORICAL MEETING PLACE

The community has always played a central role at eBay. In 1996, Omidyar added the Bulletin Board, in the hope that it would limit his role and place more of the administrative tasks of the company in the hands of the community. He no longer had the time to answer individual queries on shipping, HTML code or give advice on selling.

He wasn't disappointed. Soon questions were flooding onto the Bulletin Board. And more importantly, the answers were flooding right back. "If someone came on and said, 'please help me,' there were 25 people who would rush to help," Steven Phillips, a retired naval officer who sold chintz and pottery on the site in the early days, has recalled. Phillips used to receive

100–150 emails a day from his fellow users and would make the effort to answer every single one.[54]

A core group of regular chat room residents emerged as the pseudo customer services department. There was even a list of email addresses making it easier for users to communicate directly with the experts. Some helpful regulars began to develop personalities on the Bulletin Board.

One such regular called himself Uncle Griff. He liked answering technical questions and often referred to himself in the third person. Uncle thinks you should do this, Uncle recommends that. On asked what he looked like by a board member, he replied: "I'm wearing a lovely flower print dress and I just got through milking the cows."[55]

Uncle Griff was called Jim Griffith. After bidding on computer parts on an online trading site called AuctionWeb, he became addicted. He struggled with depression and spent some time away from the Bulletin Board. That was, until he received a phone call from Jeff Skoll, from AuctionWeb HQ, wanting to offer him a part-time position in the site's first customer-support role.

While Griffith remained Uncle Griff in the Bulletin Board, he also became dale@ebay.com to answer customer support email. Aside from offering advice, Griffith often found himself wading in to solve heated disputes between buyers and sellers. These confrontations were often taken incredibly seriously. Often he got email from eBayers saying they had cried all night, sometimes all week, because of disputes on Bulletin Boards.[56]

Griffith was soon joined by another Bulletin Board celebrity called Aunt Patti who adopted louise@ebay.com as her customer services persona. Unlike Jeff Skoll and Pierre Omidyar, Jim Griffith is still involved, 10 years later, with the day-to-day running of eBay as its Dean of Education. He still makes celebrity appearances in eBay's chat rooms, on eBay radio and at eBay live!.

Today, with 250 million global members, it's much harder for eBay to retain its community feel. It's no longer a village, but a whole nation. EBay management attempts to artificially recreate the closeness of the community from the early days, but it's almost impossible.

In 2007, eBay Live! attracted 11,000 eBayers to Boston, and in 2006, 15,000 devotees flocked to Las Vegas. EBay Live! is an annual event that enables eBayers to meet one another and meet eBay employees. It's an essential event in the calendar for eBay's management because it's a chance for them to listen and learn from their customers.

Similarly, eBay corporate offices around the world organize special "vision" days, where they invite powersellers and regular buyers into their local offices to share ideas and make suggestions. It's not the same as someone emailing Omidyar to request a change in the early days, but it's a start.

IT'S WHO YOU KNOW

The importance of communities to successful, vibrant online networks is growing. While eBay realized over 10 years ago that nurturing its community was the key to profitable and sustainable growth, a number of younger companies like MySpace and FaceBook are learning to tap into social networking.

These social networking sites are becoming a cultural phenomenon. Young people, who may be socially awkward and self-conscious in the real world, are fluent online – it's become the ideal medium for them to communicate with confidence with their peers.

MySpace is currently the web's most popular social networking site. Especially favoured among teenagers, it enables users to post details, opinions and blogs on the site. In 2005, MySpace was bought, along with its parent company, by Rupert Murdoch's News Corporation for $580m. It now has over 80 million members.

A Scottish singer called Sandi Thom made headlines in the

UK when she had a number one single, 'I wish I was a punk rocker (with flowers in my hair).' Her success was largely due to the free webcasts she broadcast from her basement in South London via her MySpace site. Although she wasn't an unsigned singer, her method of promotion made thousands of people believe they'd discovered a new and real pop star.

There are also a number of online shrines that have emerged on MySpace. When 17-year-old Anna Svidersky was stabbed to death in a small-town American restaurant, her friends composed an online tribute on the site. Suddenly, thousands of people were mourning a girl they had never met. Many began making video tributes to Anna and posting them online. One video tribute has already been watched over one million times. There is even a 200-word entry on Anna's life at Wikipedia, complete with picture from her high school year book.

In 2004, the thinktank Citivas produced a report on the way British people had reacted to events such as Princess Diana's death. They gave the mass outpouring of grief a name, "mourning sickness" and suggested that people were making phoney emotional connections in order to feel better about themselves.

When writing about Anna's MySpace shrine in the British newspaper *The Guardian,* journalist Tim Jonze suggested that chat rooms were replacing existing structures. "In an age where chat rooms and 'virtual' friends are replacing traditional support structures such as religion and the family, the need to make emotional connections is stronger than ever, even if they are not genuine," he wrote.[57]

While eBay has provided an environment for social networking for more than a decade, the incessant chatter among its community is a by-product of its marketplace. How would eBay fare if an internet site like MySpace, which has an established community, launched its own auction or e-commerce tool? Questions like that are one reason why eBay needs to nurture and attract its next generation of eBay traders.

Chapter 6

The Lives Behind the Small Ads

"I was really surprised that the chance to advertise on my forehead would sell for more on eBay than the Virgin Mary sandwich. It probably negatively affected dating, so now I just wait until it's gone."

Andrew Fischer, from Nebraska, US

It wasn't until an articulated lorry arrived at Andrew Dudley's home that he and his wife Kirsty appreciated how quickly their young eBay business had grown. When the truck driver asked them where they kept their forklift truck, they realized it was probably time to move themselves and their six young children to the mother-in-law's to make room for the stock.

The Dudleys are just one example of hundreds of thousands of people who are able to make their full-time living from eBay. The site has revolutionized their lives. It enabled them to give up jobs they didn't enjoy. There are nearly 750,000 eBayers who make a full-time living from eBay in the US and 170,000 across Europe.

It was in January 2003 that Andrew Dudley decided to dabble on eBay. He sold two rolls of 3M masking tape at a profit almost immediately. Within six months he'd moved into premises and had dedicated his career to selling branded postal supplies to eBay traders.

Andrew and Kirsty are a young, likeable couple in their 30s with six children aged between 11 and three. Running their own business has enabled them to spend quality time with their kids, while making enough money to support them. Up until last year all the children were home educated but they've since been sent to school. "EBay is perfect for fitting around our lifestyle. We can work late at night when the kids have gone to bed," explains Dudley.

Based in the Wirral, near Liverpool, they now employ 13 people. Seven of them went to school with Andrew. He's just bought some gym equipment and set it up in the warehouse for them. During one telephone conversation in the afternoon, I speak to them while they're cycling around the peninsular along the estuary, testing out Kirsty's new bike that's just arrived from eBay.

Andrew has always been an entrepreneur. In 2000, he launched a domain-name-registering business from San Francisco and he loves to devour business books and learn from other success stories. Although he'd never used eBay before, he had a friend from Birmingham who was making money by visiting car boot sales and selling items on eBay. He'd told Andrew about how much time he spent packaging his goods. (Dudley points out that 30 percent of most eBayers' time is spent on packaging their products.)

Postalsupplies purposefully only trades branded goods and has since expanded to open offices in San Francisco and Munich. "We want to become the PayPal of packaging," declares Dudley. While his first sale was £1.99 ($3.78) for two rolls of scotch tape, his three-year-old business now makes an annual turnover of £1m ($1.9m).

Dudley still has many plans. Aside from selling on eBay, he's also going to distribute his postal supplies at the British post office, which is the third largest retail network in the UK. And as he points out: "There's only one building that eBayers cluster in every day."

The Dudley family are a textbook eBay success story. They get actively involved with the eBay community and also spend time speaking at eBay university events and sharing ideas with the UK eBay management. Dudley recently co-founded the eBay business trade body FOEB, to improve the reputation of eBay among the British press and distance the brand from accusations of fraud.

He's rarely had problems with customers, describing eBay as an "honourable business." He estimates they've banked around 1,500 cheques and only had two or three bounce. Meanwhile, he reckons just one in every 10,000 customers are difficult. "Our business would not exist without eBay. EBay has been everything to us," he says.

EBAY DREAMS

Every eBay auction hides a story. The tale of the Father Christmas going into retirement and selling his costume, the geeky comic collector who finds love and sells his collection to make room for his girlfriend, the agoraphobic shopaholic.

Every full-time entrepreneur I met at eBay University was regarded with awe and respect by the other delegates. Quietly, they all seem to hope in their heart of hearts that by selling their old vinyl collection or making a profit from clothes that their kids have outgrown, they might be able to change their lives.

EBay can represent different dreams for different people. For some, it's about being able to walk out of a hated job; for some, it's about gaining some financial independence; for some, it's about boosting the household income so their family can go on holiday.

Steve Woodward insists he's different from other eBay entrepreneurs. He purposefully chose the online auction site as a channel for his full-time career. In 1998, after spending 20 years working for the British retailer Dixons, he decided to build a business on eBay.

The fact that he worked at Dixons is relevant: the electrical store was the first to offer the British public affordable internet access. Because of this, Woodward says he understood the potential of the internet early on. "Choosing eBay was a deliberate strategy, it wasn't accidental," he says.

Like Dudley, Woodward has a large family to support. He has

eight children aged between 28 and 10, and they help him run his eBay "household superstore" business, which, he says, makes a £500,000 profit annually.

"EBay hasn't changed my life; I'm still the same person. But it has changed my lifestyle," he says, emphasizing the point by stabbing at the air with his lit cigarette. Woodward still works an eight-hour day, but now it stretches from 7am until 11pm, with time taken off in the middle to spend with his family.

Woodward won the eBay umbrella during the first session of EBay University for his 39,000 feedback rating. It was the highest in the room. A stocky, balding man with a "Donald Duck" tattoo on one arm, and a "Steve and Sue" tattoo on the other, Woodward is proudly wearing his "corporate" T-shirt, in the hope of drumming up some more business. His T-shirt has his three different businesses emblazoned on the front – Parcel2Send, Astrobits and Grip N' Seal.

It's batteries that make Woodward most of his money. He reckons he packs around 5,000 items a week and sends out 6,000 emails a day to promote his business. The most important day in his eBay career was four years ago when he passed the VAT threshold and registered as a limited company.

His worst eBay customer experiences always lie in the big gap between expectation and reality. He explains: "Fifteen years ago, you'd see CDs advertising on TV with the words, 'please allow 28 days for delivery.' Today, they expect products to arrive immediately. Often customers email me and tell me how to run my business."

Jon from All Sorts is a much quieter eBay entrepreneur than Steve Woodward. But he's still got a lot to say about the brand. Towards the end of our conversation he spontaneously breaks into song. It's by "Weird Al" Yankovic and it's called "I bought on eBay." Everyone else seems to know the words too. It's a surreal moment. I'm surrounded by eBay fanatics on a pavement in central London; they're singing the eBay song to me ...

The eBay Song

A used ... pink bathrobe
A rare ... mint snowglobe
A Smurf ... TV tray
I bought on eBay
My house ... is filled with this crap
Shows up in bubble wrap
Most every day
What I bought on eBay
Tell me why (I need another pet rock)
Tell me why (I got that Alf alarm clock)
Tell me why (I bid on Shatner's old toupee)
They had it on eBay
I'll buy ... your knick-knack
Just check ... my feedback
"A++!" they all say
They love me on eBay
Gonna buy (a slightly-damaged golf bag)
Gonna buy (some Beanie Babies, new with tag)
(From some guy) I've never met in Norway
Found him on eBay
I am the type who is liable to snipe you
With two seconds left to go, whoa
Got PayPal or Visa, what ever'll please
As long as I've got the dough
I'll buy ... your tchotchkes
Sell me ... your watch, please
I'll buy (I'll buy, I'll buy, I'll buy ...)
I'm highest bidder now
(Junk keeps arriving in the mail)
(From that worldwide garage sale) (Dukes Of Hazzard
ashtray)
(Hey! A Dukes Of Hazzard ashtray)
Oh yeah ... (I bought it on eBay)
Wanna buy (a PacMan Fever lunchbox)

> Wanna buy (a case of vintage tube socks)
> Wanna buy (a Kleenex used by Dr. Dre, Dr. Dre)
> (Found it on eBay)
> Wanna buy (that Farrah Fawcett poster)
> (PEZ dispensers and a toaster)
> (Don't know why … the kind of stuff you'd throw away)
> (I'll buy on eBay)
> What I bought on eBay-y-y-y-y-y-y-y-y-y

Dressed in an eBay fleece (won at EBay University in Bristol) and jeans, Jon is tall with glasses. He's been a full-time eBayer for the last two and a half years and sells an eclectic mix of products. His most popular items are false fingernails and eyelashes and karma beads. And he also sells swimming pools.

In the late 1980s, Jon was made redundant from a graphic chart manufacturer. A redundancy payment of £10,000 helped him get used to a certain lifestyle. When he was employed again he realized he needed to make an extra £50 a month. So he dabbled on eBay. He bought a £23 laminator from a local, discount store and managed to sell it for £46 on eBay. Then he bought another two. It wasn't long before he was making more money through eBay than through his full-time job.

"EBay is brilliant because it makes it so easy to set up a business. It means you don't have to fork out thousands of pounds for a shop. It's so much cheaper. EBay will design and build e-commerce sites for people," he says. Jon's wife helps him out with the business; she works from the warehouse while he works from home. He now has a total feedback rating of over 27,000.

Jon admits that he's a workaholic, almost addicted to his eBay business. He says because he sells worldwide he needs to give the impression of being there 24/7. "I can and do work till 2am or 3am sometimes. I sell worldwide and if I can reply to a query in five minutes then I've got a better chance of getting a sale," he says.

THE HOUSE OF DVDS

Dr Steve W is a regular attendee on the EBay University powerseller panel. The other delegates love hearing how he built up his multi-million pound DVD business on eBay. Steve is called Dr Steve W because he has two PhDs, one in clinical psychology and one in social psychology. "I was a sucker for education," he says. One of his dissertations examined the psychology of loss of faith.

After his PhDs, Dr Steve W worked as a clinical psychologist. During a period spent profiling for the Home Office, he met the serial killer Ian Brady, who murdered five children in Lancashire in the mid 1960s, "the most evil person I'd ever met." Then somehow, he worked as a management consultant, specializing in telecoms. Then he "blagged" his way into Arthur Andersen in New York.

During a powerseller panel, Dr Steve W has the audience enthralled as he tells them that being in New York on 9/11 inspired him to change his life and set up an eBay business. He later admits that following the Enron scandal he and his friends were waiting to be made redundant from the troubled Andersen business. "Our problem was that we didn't like working for other people," he reveals.

Dr Steve W returned to the UK and, after taking a wrong turning during a car journey, found himself at a DVD wholesaler. He managed to blag his way in and bought just seven DVDs of horror films that he resold on eBay. That was March 1 2002, and today the same wholesaler buys its DVDs from Steve's company.

Dr Steve W's business is run from his house. He doesn't have a warehouse, which means he shares his home with 270,000 DVDs and CDs. "There isn't a room in the house, aside from the bathroom, that isn't stacked with them," he laughs. "I spend a lot of time in the bath; it's hard to wind down."

He was supposed to be getting an extension, but the first plans were rejected, and six months were gone. And then his builder went to Egypt for Christmas and caught salmonella. So now there's another delay.

Dr Steve W employs seven people in total, two of whom work part-time. They include his ex-wife Jean and a lady called Karen, who crops up regularly during his life story – they have been engaged four times.

Dr Steve W's business makes an annual turnover of around £7.5m ($14m), and he says 10 percent of this comes from eBay, the rest from his own website and selling direct to wholesalers. EBay has helped to grow his business because of its global reach. He has different eBay stores in different countries all over the world. One man in Australia buys 50 DVDs from him every month.

"EBay helped me make a living. It's not that clever but it's made me realize that I don't want to work for other people any more," he says. "EBay appeals to people because the idea of selling something is terrifying. But it gives people a chance to dabble and see how they'd get on with it."

BEING UNEMPLOYABLE

Chris's local post office loves him. They make him cups of tea and worry if he doesn't turn up. As a full-time eBayer, Chris is normally in the post office every day. He decided to develop an eBay business when he was made redundant from a sales job. He needed to pay his mortgage.

He helped a friend sell some Herman Miller chairs on eBay, and they split the profits. Then he thought, "Why bother looking for another job?" and "kind of fell into" online auctioneering. Today, Chris makes around £8,000 a month selling second hand computer parts on eBay. With a smile, he describes his profit margins as "obscene"; triple digit. The previous week, he'd sold two printers bought for £5 each for £300 each on eBay.

Chris says he doesn't need to employ anyone else. He works from home and stores his stock in an old stable block. If he sets his mind to it, he can finish his day's work by midday and go and play a round of golf with his brother, secure in the knowledge his business won't suffer.

"EBay pays me almost as much as my last job for a lot less effort. There's no stress; I can take a day off whenever I want. Yes, eBay has changed my life," he says. Like many other eBayers, Chris says he'll never return to the corporate world. "I'm unemployable," he laughs. He's relieved that most of his stock is bought by either small businesses or larger corporates; it means he's not attracting "numpty buyers." Who? "People who just don't know," he replies.

Chris is loyal to eBay, but only because it makes business sense. The other smaller sites don't attract the buyers he needs. "I buy products; eBay buys customers. If eBay fails to find me customers then I've got no problem going elsewhere," he says.

Sean Coolness was attracted to eBay because of his marriage. He'd settled down and was thinking of having kids but he was a workaholic. "I'd already seen one marriage go down the pan," he reveals. So he left his job as an IT manager and set up a full-time business selling books, bikes and computers on eBay. Now he works from home so he can "spend more time with the missus and kids."

Sean says he earns enough to pay the bills but suggests that it's hard to make good money on eBay. "You've got to be a dedicated business person. I'm not 100 percent business driven, so I don't maximize everything I could," he admits.

Sean believes in the eBay community. He's learnt to trust strangers, and they've learned to trust him. When he first launched his eBay business he was selling a motorcycle with a broken indicator, broken clutch and no MOT. The winner of the auction emailed him to see if he would be able to ride it home. Sean decided to MOT the bike for him.

The buyer travelled over 450 miles from his home in Glasgow to southern England to collect the bike, and Sean collected him from the train station. The buyer paid Sean the extra cash for the MOT. "I thought he was stark raving mad," recalls Sean. "But it shows the power of the feedback system. He decided he could ride it home purely on the strength of other people's opinions."

EQUAL OPPORTUNITIES

Steve Woodward wants me to talk to his wife, Donna. She's grown to become a powerseller with 3,500 feedback in just a year. She's tall, dressed in denim cut-off jeans, a denim jacket and a branded T-Shirt. With a long brown plait swinging behind her, she wears lots of gothic silver jewellery, including a skull necklace.

She's able to run her business around her kids. So she scales it down during the summer holidays and scales it up again the rest of the year. She sells celtic and gothic jewellery and cigarette lighters. She says she has lots of regulars, especially the lighter collectors.

EBay offers a family-friendly income stream for many women. It enables them to get back to work and balance earning money with childcare. Most eBayers can work from home and also choose the hours they work – when the kids are at school or in bed.

Angie Matthews comes from Norwich in the east of England, dubbed the eBay capital of the UK. She has two young children, and eBay gave her the lifeline she needed when she was getting bored after a year of spending time with her kids.

"I needed adult stuff," she explains. "If there's a crisis at home I can log off. It means I can work around the kids from home." It's getting harder since her eight-month-old baby started crawling but her fledgling eBay business has built up her confidence again.

Matthews is a spiritual healer. She sells crystals and woodcarvings on eBay and has built up a feedback rating of around 2,000. Wearing tinted glasses and a purple, crochet cardigan she's excited to be socializing with her eBay friends. She's made good friends with other eBayers, but also with some of her customers. Sometimes, she'll add a note to her package to make it more personal for customers. And sometimes her eBay customers will come to her for spiritual healing as well.

EBAY ADDICTION

There's something very addictive about eBay. Buyers don't buy an item, they win it. EBay addiction has always been a running joke among the community but the thrill of the auction is compelling. It's easy to see how eBayers might buy products they don't want or don't need purely to experience the rush of winning.

In the early days in 1999, eBay held an "eBay addicts" competition where users emailed their stories of reliance on the online auction site. There were emails about being two hours late for work because of searching for something on eBay, emails about the joy of a boyfriend falling fast asleep so they could creep back downstairs and turn the computer back on.

The winner was a woman who sold toys on eBay and described how eBay had taken over her life. "My husband became concerned and kept saying I was addicted to eBay! 'No way,' I would say, as I stepped over the neglected dead carcasses of our cats!"[58]

However, eBay addiction today is a recognizable medical disorder. Clinical psychologist Dr Kimberly Young is an expert on internet addiction, based in Bradford, in the US. She splits internet addiction into five different categories – cybersexual addiction, cyberrelationship addiction, net compulsions, information overload and computer addiction. While cybersexual addiction is the most common form, Young found online auction addiction occurred in 15 percent of the cases she studies.

Through her practice, the Center for Online Addiction, Young treats eBay addicts through telephone and online counselling. She believes that eBay addiction has increased over the last few years and is this century's example of shopping addiction. Young meets patients who have become so addicted to eBay that they fall into debt, need to take out a second mortgage or even bankrupt themselves.

Dr Young runs a short test on her website *www.netaddiction.com* for eBayers to test whether they're overly dependent on online auction houses. Users need to answer yes or no to the following statements.

1. Do you need to bid with increasing amounts of money in order to achieve the desired excitement?
2. Are you preoccupied with auction houses (thinking about being online when offline, anticipating your next online session)?
3. Have you lied to friends and family members to conceal the extent of your online bidding?
4. Do you feel restless or irritable when attempting to cut down or stop online bidding?
5. Have you made repeated unsuccessful efforts to control, cut back, or stop online bidding?
6. Do you use auction houses as a way of escaping from problems or relieve feelings of helplessness, guilt, anxiety or depression?
7. Have you jeopardized or lost a significant relationship, job or educational or career opportunity because of online bidding?
8. Have you committed illegal acts such as forgery, fraud, theft or embezzlement to finance online activities?

HUSBANDS, WIVES AND LOVERS

Although eBay addiction touches on the dark side of the online auction site, it's also an online location that reverberates with pranks, jokes and laughter. There have been husbands, mothers and love rats all put up for sale on eBay. Auctioning risqué pictures of ex-girlfriends has also become a popular pursuit among jilted lovers.

One seller, known as Baldie278, put up pictures of his ex Sarah in a bikini and underwear as revenge. On the site he wrote, "Here's to you Sarah! Enjoy the rest of your life with Brad. Hope everyone else enjoys you as well!"[59]

Once, an angry bride auctioned her mother on eBay to make sure she didn't turn up at her wedding. In her ad she wrote: "My mother is for sale, in the hope that someone will buy her and keep her away from our wedding as she has promised to ruin it. All I want is for them to leave me alone and let me have my wedding in peace. Please stop her ruining my wedding."

When the mother had been told she wasn't welcome at her daughter's wedding, she'd hired a private investigator to find out when it was scheduled. After he'd made successful enquiries, the daughter twice moved the wedding venue, date and time. As a last resort, she decided to sell her mother on eBay. However, eBay removed the listing – twice.[60]

Men get sold on eBay too. A husband has been put up for sale on eBay – by his wife. Nadia Manfroid, a 21-year-old from Brussels, Belgium, wanted time away from her husband Denis, but didn't want him to be on his own.

Meanwhile, in the UK, a Sunday league football team auctioned their friend Steve Bundock on eBay because they were sick of him stealing their girlfriends. They listed him on eBay, writing he was, "no longer required by friends due to trust and reliability issues," adding that he, "cannot be left unsupervised with a girlfriend, sister or gran." Bundock received six bids, the highest for £156 before eBay pulled the plug on the auction because "the goods are not deliverable."[61]

THE TATTOO MAN

Some savvy eBayers are able to make both fame and money by auctioning quirky items on the auction site. Goldenpalace, a Canadian casino, is one company that enjoys bidding for wacky items on eBay.

It's a savvy marketing strategy that exploits the press's voracious appetite for the weird and wonderful. Jeff Kay, Goldenpalace's marketing director, says his brand has been boosted by sales including Britney Spear's pregnancy test, the Pope's car and an opportunity to advertise on a pregnant stomach. "The power of the eBay brand is amazing. They are the Coca-Cola of what they do. When you say auction, you say eBay," he explains.

One of Goldenpalace's successful purchases is Andrew Fischer, a 22-year-old from Omaka, Nebraska, who auctions his forehead on eBay. The winner gets to tattoo their logo onto his head for 30 days. And in just two months he has made $50,000 from his new business.

"It can be quite annoying walking around with a tattoo on your head for 30 days because everyone stares at you. But I'm getting used to it," he muses. "I was really surprised that the chance to advertise on my forehead would sell for more on eBay than the cheese sandwich that looked like the Virgin Mary."

Fischer was working for a company that was a powerseller on eBay. So he already spent all day, every day on the auction site and understood how some crazy items became incredibly popular. Within four days, he was getting calls from the local media, then the national media picked up on the story and it snowballed from there. He says he was picky about what he wanted on his forehead. He turned down the bids from several adult entertainment sites.

BABY BRANDING

For sale: A newborn baby

30 May 2005

13 bids

Winning bid: $999.99

This auction is for ad space on our newborn son for 1 month. By ad space I mean only on clothing/ Tshirts or any other type of apparel like hats, shoes....ect. You can also put your ad on a stroller or anything else that is baby related and send it to us. The winner of this auction will be responsible for making up and sending us the clothing and any apparel that we will putting on our son. The clothing will need to be 0–3 months boy summer clothing. WE WILL NOT TATOO ANYTHING EVEN TEMP TATOOS ON OUR SON SO DO NOT ASK. ANYTHING THAT IS SENT TO US FOR OUR SON MUST BE FIT FOR A BOY, IN OTHER WORDS WE WILL NOT PUT ANYTHING GIRLY ON HIM LIKE A DRESS OR ANYTHING LIKE THAT.

Fischer lives in the middle of nowhere and he enjoys the month when he's sporting a forehead tattoo; it means he's constantly travelling around and visiting different TV studios. He'd really like to become an actor and is using some of the money to take classes.

However, he has noticed that having a tattooed forehead is not great for meeting girls. "It's probably negatively affected dates," he sighs. "Now I wait until it's gone. People feel awkward just being with you …"

Chapter 7

Selling My Soul on eBay

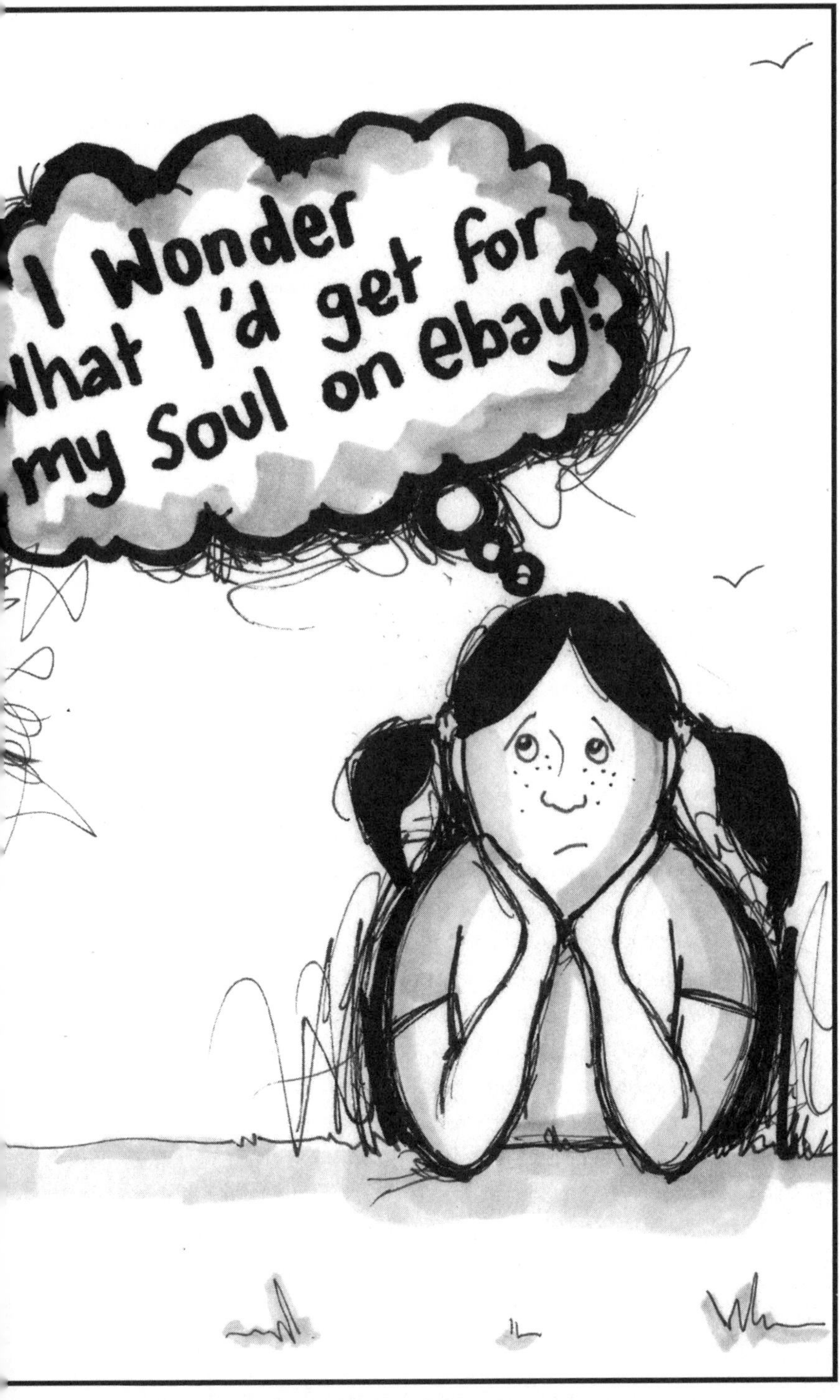
I Wonder What I'd get for my Soul on ebay?

Winning bid: £101.00

Ended: 05-Jul-06 22:00:00 BST
Postage costs: Free
Collection in Person (more services)
Post to: Worldwide
Item location: twickenham, Middlesex, United Kingdom
History: 14 bids
Winning bidder: c993 (142 ☆)

Meet the seller

Seller: elliepaynter (
10 ☆) me
Feedback: 100% Positive
Member: since 02-Sep-05
in United Kingdom

▪ Read feedback comments
▪ Ask seller a question
▪ Add to Favourite Sellers
▪ View seller's other items

Some people are born to run eBay auctions, and some are not. It requires strength of will, a calm disposition, a laissez-faire attitude and the awareness of what makes a good sale. Some of us are better suited to the role of eBay shopper, where we can flit and browse, watch an item and forget about it, bid on something and walk away or stealthily bid at the last minute for a coveted item.

On Sunday June 25 2006 at 10pm I launched an eBay auction for this chapter. The bids began at 99p, and I promised to tell the winner's eBay story in my book, donating proceeds to charity. It was an idea that enabled me to use the subject of my narrative as a writing tool. It was also a chance for an eBay toe-dipper to dive into the deep end. A chance for a writer to stop observing and reporting, and participate.

It had never been done before. Stephen King, the American horror novelist had auctioned the opportunity to name a character for charity. And a budding novelist called Phil McArthur wrote a collaborative thriller with the help of eBay. The novel was written one page at a time, one writer to a page. As each instalment was finished, the next was offered for auction on eBay. While the writing was a patchwork of styles and tones, there's no shortage of plot.

But nobody had ever auctioned a whole chapter before. It sounds ridiculous, but it took days to write the description. What category does a chapter fall into on eBay? There may be 50,000 different categories available, but there's not one for book chapters. There was one for books though, so I popped it in there; just in case a bookworm decided they wanted to star in a book as well as buy or read one.

Then, of course, there's the infamous "everything else" category. It's the home for useless husbands, pictures of ex-girlfriends in their underwear, diet pills, penis enlargers and a myriad of money-making schemes, including the rather intriguing "£70,000 a month profit or we'll give you £25,000." There was even an ex-air hostess prepared to flog the secrets of free air travel for the right price, which happened to be £4.95.

So the auction for chapter seven of *The eBay Phenomenon* found a slightly unnatural home nestled among "everything else," under "services." It was also listed in non-fiction books under marketing and communications. This took it away from the eBay money-making guides and the celebrity biographies, into a slightly more cerebral category. There was nowhere else it seemed to fit.

EBay's categories are a common source of fierce debate between management and the community. In the early days especially, collectors would conduct fiery discussions with eBay's team about what should and should not constitute a new category. An exasperated button collector attempted to explain the fine differences between sewing collectibles and vintage buttons; while radio specialists would endeavour to educate eBay about Bakelite vintage radios.

Finally, after crafting my 250 word entry, I framed it in cascading, multi-coloured books, taken from one of eBay's design templates. Then it was just a question of sitting and waiting. For 10 whole days.

THE BOOK AUCTION

I'm an English author and journalist writing a book on the eBay phenomenon to be published by Cyan Books this autumn. <u>I will tell the story of the winner of this auction in chapter seven of my book.</u> The working title of my book is *Great Brand Stories: eBay, the brand that taught millions of people to trust one another.*

<u>This is a genuine opportunity to appear in a book that will be published globally.</u> My last book on the Swedish Furniture store Ikea, called *Great Ikea!: A brand for all the people* was listed in the top five business books of the year, by the English newspaper *The Times*. (See picture below.) It has since been published in the UK and Sweden, and will soon be published in China, Korea, Spain, Russia and America.

I will travel to interview you and retell your story in my book. I will need to meet you within a few weeks of the auction ending, in order to hit my deadline. The rest of the proceeds for this auction will be donated to a charity called Book Aid International, which distributes books in developing countries. http://www.bookaid.org

You can check my credentials in my About Me page and also on my website www.elenlewis.com. You will also be able to see information on my writing by typing 'Elen Lewis' into Google. As well as writing books I've written for newspapers such as *The Financial Times* and *The Guardian*. I also used to be the editor of a magazine about marketing called *Brand Strategy*. For details of my last book, *Great Ikea!: A Brand for all the people*, see Amazon.

Please do get in touch if you've got any queries.

On June 26, just one day after listing somebody called anglismutuel matched the reserve price of 99p. But who was she or he and what was her story? Without an "about me" page, it's impossible to get a sense of someone's history.

Despite dedicated detective work, the only available information was that anglismutuel joined eBay on November 4 2002 and had a feedback rating of 61. It's very difficult to discern much about eBay users from their username. It's like the Tower of Babel. There are girls with boys' names and boys called cider! or auctionmydog.

EBay enables its community to create an identity all of their own. It's a chance to dump the name you hate, cloak yourself in anonymity and adopt the online persona you've always dreamt of. An introverted, agoraphobic can transform themselves into "brazilian cookie," a larger-than-life personality who tap dances in and out of the eBay chat rooms. A shy loner with a stutter called John Smith can waltz around eBay soliloquizing and call himself "oldmanfunk."

All the world's names are here, and the rest. Squiffsmummy, lilac-mist, mad*woman, joiseychick, misswhiplash27, hollywoodstarlet and rooobarbcustard. The bidders in my auction were comparatively conservative: coolkit, owlsie2005, billpilkington, crusoeboe and c993.

After a whole week of limbo, where it looked as if anglismutuel might secure their name in fame for just £1.04, the auction heated up. Over 270 eBayers had checked out the auction, a small number compared with eBay's biggest auctions; and then a powerseller called coolkit pushed the price up to £9.42 and then £24.00. At £26.00, anglismutuel bowed out, a controlled buyer who obviously sticks to a budget.

Then, an email from someone called wallaceandgrommit2003 dropped into my in-box, see below. His real name was Bill Pilkington, wallaceandgrommit was his eBay name. The email was brief and included a mobile phone number. I called and left a long rambling message clogging up his voice mail. Then I emailed.

```
    From:  Bill
 Subject:  RE: ?????????????
    Date:  4 July 2006
      To:  Elen
```

Hi,

An interesting auction you have. My only concern is: is
the sale genuine?

There are one or two alarm bells ringing.

Please feel free to call me (normal 9.00am-10.30pm please.

Regards

Bill

On the evening of July 5, a fluttering swarm of butterflies battled in my stomach. Fixated on the eBay auction nothing had happened for hours. At 17:17pm, owlsie2005 bid £32.50 then all was quiet. It was silent for nearly five hours. It was like playing hide and seek, and hiding and waiting and holding your breath until someone found you.

Then, faster than the page could be refreshed, it was all over. And in the space of just two minutes, the value of the auction had leapt from £32.50 to £101.00. It was all thanks to a process called sniping, one of the most controversial areas of buying practice on eBay. Sniping involves specially-developed software that enables bidders to buy an item right at the last minute. It's the equivalent of shouting out a final bid just before the auctioneer's hammer hits the table.

Sniping on eBay was invented in 1997 by an American called David Eccles. Initially, he would snipe by hand, typing in a bid just as an auction was about to end, but then he decided to write some sniping software. He taught himself to write a programme that was tuned into eBay's official clock and enabled bidders to bid in the final seconds of an auction and called it Cricket Jr.

Soon he was selling nearly 400 copies of his sniping software monthly to eBayers, for $10 each. He was promptly joined by a flurry of competitors selling similar software. One survey of 1,000 auctions found that of those with more than one bid, 18 percent were won in the last 60 seconds.

Some eBayers don't approve of sniping. They say it's unfair. It does mean that often items are sold to the buyer who most deftly plays the system, rather than the buyer who is willing to spend the most. Unlike other auction sites, which automatically extend the bidding process if someone bids in the final few minutes, eBay has not altered its model.

Instead, it encourages individuals to use something called proxy bidding. Bidders can enter the maximum price they're prepared to pay for an item, and eBay will then bid on their behalf to automatically keep them as the top bidder. EBay insists that this renders sniping redundant, as proxy bidders only ever lose to snipers who bid more than their maximum bid.

Sniping is interesting because it raises questions about how much of a level playing field eBay really is. "It's only when an inexperienced buyer learns the tricks that they can really compete," explains David A. Karp, author of *eBay Hacks*.

A PROFESSIONAL AUCTIONEER

The winner of my auction was c993, whose bid of £101.00 arrived just two seconds before the hammer signalled the end of the auction. He was called Christian Braun and had intended to bid from the beginning. When he decided to check out the auction on Wednesday evening, there were just 10 seconds left.

Like most of the bidders on the auction, Braun makes a professional living from eBay but used his personal identity to bid. He is the 38-year-old founder and CEO of a British business called Auctioning4u. It's one of many companies clustered on the periphery of the eBay effect that's cashing in on supporting the auction site's community.

Auctioning4u felt like a business of our era. In today's modern, busy environment, time is our most precious commodity. And selling stuff on eBay can be a real chore. The listing, the packing, responding to respective buyer's queries – it's not ideal for time-stretched professionals who'd like to make some money by clearing out their attics.

Auctioning4u had five "drop-off" points scattered around London. It could also collect items from London or send a courier. Busy executives can dump their unwanted clutter and leave Auctioning4u to sell their items on eBay, in exchange, of course, for a cut of the final price. Braun described his business in simple terms: "EBay is a stock exchange and we're a business trader."

In 2006, Auctioning4u sold around 150 items a day, and Braun said it would sell 1,000 daily by 2007. It generated £300,000 a month in 2006; a figure that Braun said would increase ten fold by 2007. At any one time, the business sold 35,000 items with most listings lasting six and a half days on average.

THE EBAY CONVEYOR BELT

As a full-time eBay seller, Auctioning4u has developed the listing and packing process into a fine art. Items move through its system smoothly as if on an imaginary conveyor belt. They arrive at the warehouse from its collection vans, other shops or are dropped off by customers. Reception checks the items and takes them into a section of the warehouse to be listed on eBay and photographed.

Auctioning4u often prepares items for sale. This process could involve carefully washing an antique china set or stripping the software and content from laptops. Items are organized into five categories: fashion, electrical goods, general stuff, collectibles or larger products and furniture. Each item is given a special bar code, so Auctioning4u's software can track the location of its products.

The company employs a number of part-time specialists to write knowledgeable product descriptions for eBay. They work in the same room as a photographer, who captures the items in professional photo stations with a plain backdrop and reflectors to create the right lighting.

There will be no humorous photos among Auctioning4u's items, which is probably a shame for the rest of us. Then again, there's only so many pictures of naked men captured in the reflection of a shiny kettle or a TV screen that you can take.

Next, the items are moved into the cavernous warehouse and taken to join their peers on a special shelf or area. After an average wait of about seven days, they are packaged and posted to their new home. The packing area in the warehouse is full of rolls of brown paper, bubble wrap and masking tape. On busy days, the company can pack and ship 250 items a day; on quieter days, it's more like 150. And every day at 4pm the postal van rolls up to collect the packages.

ARE YOU THE PROUD OWNER OF THINGS THAT COLLECT DUST?

Auctioning4u is located in a grim, industrial area in London called North Acton. Its warehouse and headquarters are sandwiched between an interminably busy ring road and the contrasting oasis of an ancient cemetery, where the first British airman to fly upside down is buried.

At first glance, Auctioning4u seems to be sharing its car park with the Post Office, if the bright red postal van is anything to go by. And for a start-up, it also seems to employ a high number of people with an expensive taste in cars. But first impressions are deceptive. I discover later that the postal van is for sale, along with most of the other cars parked outside. There are also two collection vans outside, branded in Auctioning4u's pink and grey colours. "Are you the proud owner of things that collect dust?" the company asks, before answering, "Be the proud owner of cash instead."

Inside the warehouse, some offices are being carved out of the cavernous space, with management sitting upstairs at a group of desks that barely fills the new room. All conversations are punctuated with bangs, crashes and drilling. Today, the carpet has been laid, and another 15 desks have been ordered. Then the building rattles as a train speeds past.

The interconnecting warehouse is like an Aladdin's cave for the online marketplace. Brown masking tape dividing the floor and some shelves hint at a system among the chaos. A French antique flowery sofa, tupperware containers of mobile phones, exercise bikes and a mannequin jostle for space with a drum kit, two white bird cages and some washing machines.

Imagine all the flotsam and jetsam listed on eBay safely housed in the real-world location of North Acton, London, and you'll get a good idea of Auctioning4u. Vintage radios and power tools, golf clubs and trampolines, oxygen tanks, guitars, Burberry macs and Gucci handbags, red velvet curtains and oversized, peach, silk roses. It's all here. And more, including a giant Wallace and Gromit poster and a bright pink, stripy candy floss stall.

The most expensive item Auctioning4u has ever sold on eBay was a fully-restored Ford Mustang Shelby. The eBay listings intricately detailed every element of the car; they even included a sound file with the roar of the engine. It was sold for £85,000 to an American collector. Once he had arranged for the shipper to come and confirm that the car actually existed, he transferred the money immediately, and the car was shipped to the US. One of the most unusual items was a 20 metre Mongolian Yurt; it was the largest yurt outside Mongolia and had its own 7.5 tonne container.

Christian Braun believes that Auctioning4u's expertise often enables items to sell for more than they would do if the owner listed them on eBay themselves. He cites the example of a collectible toy car that fetched £17.60. When Auctioning4u took the sale on, it listed it in the correct category and included a picture of the car's box. This time, it sold again for £68.

Auctioning4u's selling business is split into four parts – they sell about one quarter fashion items, one quarter electronics, one quarter collectibles and one quarter other stuff. Its sellers are a mixed bunch, but what they do have in common is that they don't buy or sell on eBay, perhaps because they're too busy, or because they don't like using the internet. A few years ago, they might have gone to car boot sales.

Auctioning4u even has some regular buyers through its shop on eBay. One customer in Belgium used to buy around 10 different items a day. Another bought 100 products last week. Sometimes, these customers turn into sellers too; they have to ask Auctioning4u to sell stuff for them because they've bought too much.

THE TIMPO TOYS CLUB

Despite the sweltering day and the building mayhem in his office, Braun is dressed formally in a white short sleeved shirt, trousers and leather shoes. He clutches his mobile phone and a clipboard with sheets of blank white paper under his arm as he strides across the cemetery to reach our lunch destination. We sit outside what may be the only café in North Acton, shaded from the blazing sun under orange parasols and sheltered from a busy road and industrial estate by a trellis trailing sweet peas.

When Christian Braun was growing up near Düsseldorf, Germany, he learnt to appreciate the dynamics of supply and demand; an economics lesson that would bear him in good stead as he built a business trading on eBay 20 years later. He was still at school when he began selling and buying vintage toys to earn pocket money.

From the age of 15, Braun would hitchhike around his local area to buy old toys gathering dust on the shelves of newsagents and sell them on for a profit to collectors. He even printed and distributed a special price list. It was the only guide that existed for Timpo Toys collectors, and soon they were swapping according to the "Braun price list."

In hindsight, it made perfect sense for Braun to launch a business to help collectors exchange their items more easily. But when he first had the idea for Auctioning4u he wanted to find someone else to run the business for him. "I had two or three people who I thought were best suited to the job. They liked the power of the idea, but it wasn't their baby," he explains.

By this point, Braun had been working for some time as a venture capitalist. I ask if this is why he wanted to get someone else to run the business for him, rather than get involved himself. "Yes, I suppose it's the VC in you," he admits. "You can do more things if you get other people involved and I just wanted a stake in it."

It seems unlikely now, as Braun chats fluently away in his second language English, but when he was at school, languages were his weak point. He nearly had to re-sit an academic year at the age of 11 because his English was so bad. Today, he can speak French and a little Spanish, and his wife is Russian, so he can probably speak a bit of that as well. (They met at The Hermitage museum in St Petersburg.)

Braun's proficiency in languages is probably because he has travelled extensively during his working career. Aside from the UK and Germany, he has lived, worked or studied in Hong Kong, Warsaw, Moscow, St Petersburg, Ukraine, and Stanford and New York in the US. He first lived abroad during his degree, when he decided he wanted to study internationally. At the age of just 23 he did an MBA at the London Business School; he was the second youngest in his year.

In his first proper job he worked as a junior partner at a mergers and acquisitions boutique in Moscow. He helped to grow the young company from 0-60 people and regularly commuted between Moscow and St Petersburg on a night train. He would board the train at Moscow at midnight, arriving at St Petersburg at 8am. After a day in the office, he would make the same journey in reverse, boarding the train at midnight and arriving in time for work in Moscow the following morning.

But when the crisis between Russia and Chechnya escalated in 1999, Braun was forced to close down the business. "The foreign investors stopped coming," he recalls. So he joined global management consultancy firm Bain and Co, where he was based in Ukraine, helping foreign companies enter the market.

Perhaps it was here that the seeds of launching his own company were sown. Although he was paid more money to live in Ukraine, he didn't enjoy it. "I don't see the point of working for someone else. I was getting paid 'bush money' but life's too short. In the same way, I wouldn't work on an oil platform for someone else. I wanted to get out," he recalls.

Life in Ukraine was tough for expats in many different ways. There was an ongoing, grinding struggle to sort out the simplest tasks that most of us take for granted in more developed countries. For example, in Braun's apartment, the heating would only be switched on if the temperature dropped below zero. And frequently, when temperatures were freezing at -5 or -8, Braun would become trapped in circular discussions with his landlord, who insisted it was above freezing and there was no need for heating.

So Braun moved to the US, working at GE Capital. He stayed here for five years, again moving around the globe from Cologne to Warsaw, to London, to Atlanta and Stanford, collecting businesses along the way. In his final position at General Electric, he was working as a VC in the equity arm, heading the financial services and software team.

THE PULL OF SECOND-HAND MARKETS

Around 2002, Braun and his wife started to dabble with an auction site called eBay. They used it to sell a Canon digital camera for £40. Braun was intrigued. Since his childhood when he traded Timpo toys to earn extra pocket money, he'd always been interested in second-hand markets. He says he's drawn to the elegance and craftsmanship of old stuff.

Braun's wife began to sell more things on eBay. By 2003, she was helping her friends profit as they cleared out their cellars and attics. She and Braun even visited antique dealers on Portobello Road in London and began to sell some of their stock on eBay for them. The idea was gaining momentum, and Braun knew he had to launch a business before someone else did.

When he failed to persuade any of his contacts to run the business for him, Braun knew he had no choice but to step up to the task himself. It was time to move to the other side of the table – from investor to entrepreneur. In December 2003, he was drawing on all his contacts to raise angel funding for the new venture. He spoke to over 150 people and managed to raise capital.

Braun's angel investors included Christopher Sharples, former chairman of the Securities and Futures Authority, and Patrick Folkes, who founded PJ Smoothies. Auctioning4u officially launched in 2004.

Since then, Braun has assembled his management team, who have all invested in the company. His recruitment process seems rigorous. He asked them each for 30 references, and gave them the same in return. "By enabling management to own part of the business I've attracted a better calibre of people," he says. He still owns around one third of the company, though.

Braun is aggressively growing the company. He has made three acquisitions of smaller, similar businesses, which enabled him to acquire new contacts and sell their inventory through

Auctioning4u. In May 2006, he raised £2.25m in funding from VC firm Foresight Venture Partners and existing investors. "It's OK being small or large, but the middle ground is tough," he says. But isn't this the territory that Auctioning4u occupies? "Yes, we're in the middle," he admits. "But we're growing fast."

GROWING UP

Braun equates his business model with a power plant. He says it's not enough for Auctioning4u to grow organically; it needs to grow big and it needs to grow fast. Like eBay, Auctioning4u has spotted the potential of the corporate market, which could help accelerate its growth. It already sells items for a number of corporate clients in the public sector.

"We need volume. Sometimes, it feels as if we're moving too slow," he says. It's a risky strategy, but Braun is convinced it's worthwhile. He talks in terms of huge numbers when valuing the market – as much as £150bn in the UK alone. Braun breaks this figure down: "The markets where we are the best solution available are unwanted possessions (£6bn), overstock and returns (£10bn) and collectibles (£15bn). If you add new products, the market is enormous, easily in the £150bn area."

When Auctioning4u first launched, Braun talked about opening 50-60 shops in London alone, where consumers could drop off their unwanted items to be sold on eBay. It currently has just four shops in the UK capital, and Braun niftily sidesteps a question about when precisely all the other shops will open. "When people are ready," he smiles.

If his plan comes to fruition then Auctioning4u could become as common a sight on the British high street as a drycleaners. Though Braun says they won't be quite such a commodity. "It's not a weekly need but a monthly need," he says.

If Braun's vision is realized and his brand builds a strong retail presence, it could, of course, affect the fortunes of charities.

Instead of handing over their unwanted possessions to the nearest charity shop, people will entrust them to Auctioning4u in the hope of ready cash.

The diversion of funds from charity is another potentially dark side to the eBay effect. (See Chapter Ten.) However, Auctioning4u is attempting to minimize it by helping charity shops sell their more expensive items on eBay. For a fee. It has formed partnerships with Barnardo's, Mind and Save the Children and collects donations that will sell for over £30 on eBay. The charity receives 68 percent of the final auction price, while Auctioning4u pockets the rest.

Auctioning4u's aggressive growth means it's not making any money of its own yet, though. Braun says it will break even at the end of the year, and generate profits by 2007. But what if it all goes wrong? He seems a little startled by the question. "As an entrepreneur, you can't have a fallback or an alternative," he says passionately.

Sadly, Auctioning4u went into administration in January 2008; sometimes the middle men get squeezed out of eBay's ecosystem.

Like many other businesses clustering on the periphery of the global auction house, Auctioning4u tried to capitalize on the same trends that are driving eBay's success and become another well-oiled cog in the wheel of disposable living. The concept of temporary ownership is growing in popularity; people don't buy items for life any more. When they get bored with them, they can sell them on to someone else, and start all over again.

Chapter 8

Growing Pains

> "What town has ever grown from 100,000 to two million in less than a year? We're trying to evolve and cope as best we can."
>
> **Meg Whitman**[62]

The thrill of the auction has seized the imagination of the world. No longer separated by the physical boundaries of location, budding auctioneers can trade in a global marketplace. While a Chinese eBayer carefully packages shawls for an excited winner in downtown Manhattan, a German toy collector trades items with his counterpart in New Zealand.

It's a romantic image. It's like the stuff of spice trade legends, when the world became a smaller place and Europe experienced cinnamon, cloves and pepper for the first time. It was the beginning of the modern age. From 1498, following the first direct sea voyage from Europe to Asia, when seafarers shouted, "for Christ and spices!" as they leapt ashore, suddenly a new world perspective was discovered.

And eBay has painted a fresh perspective; it has created a new global marketplace for traders. EBay has empowered villagers from developing countries to profit from selling to the "hand-bagged" glitterati of the US and Europe. It has shrunk communities of collectors into online chat rooms and boosted the traffic of brown paper parcels zig zagging the globe.

EBay has outgrown its image as America's online flea market, a specialist in PEZ dispensers and Superman lunch boxes. Indeed, since the first quarter of 2005, the number of registered eBay users abroad exceeded those at home. As the American online auction matures, its domestic growth is slowing down.

GROWING FROM A TOWN INTO A NATION

If a country grew as swiftly as eBay has in the last 10 years, it would probably crumble. There would be civil unrest as systems shut down, unable to cope with demand. As eBay's management scrabbled to assemble systems for the online auction house in the tailwind of its momentous growth it experienced problems.

In 1998, as eBay's senior team faced criticism for its slow response to an anti-fraud issue, Whitman revealed the strain of keeping up. "What town has ever grown from 100,000 to two million in less than a year? We're trying to evolve and cope as best we can."[63]

When Meg Whitman joined eBay in 1998, the online auction site had 300,000 registered users. She thought it would be great if eBay could grow to one million users and maybe one day generate $1bn in sales. In 2006, eBay had over 200 million users and generated $6bn in sales.

But today, it's also a very different business from the one launched by Pierre Omidyar in 1996. No longer a US business, eBay has become a global marketplace – present in 33 countries. No longer a pure auction business, eBay hosted 383,000 online shops on its site in 2005 and generated 34 percent of total GMV (gross merchandise value) from fixed-price sales in the final quarter of 2005.

Following its acquisitions of online payment system, PayPal, and internet telephony company, Skype, eBay is no longer in the simple e-commerce business. It is also a payment company and a telecoms company. The days of the simple mechanism to auction a laser pointer are a distant memory.

A EUROPEAN INVASION

In the beginning, eBay was unashamedly all-American. From the items it sold, to the burbling chatter on the community boards –

there was no doubt that eBay was an American brand. Ten years since launch, eBay is making its country sites as relevant to their local market as possible. But in the early days, its attempts at expansion resulted in colonies rather than a truly global business.

English-speaking Europeans were dabbling on eBay's US site, way before it expanded across the Atlantic. By 1999, its registered users came from 90 different countries. But they still felt like tourists. All message boards and auctions were conducted exclusively in English, so many of them had to talk in a foreign language. And the auctions were all being valued and run in US dollars. From culture, to language to currency eBay was a foreign destination for many of its users and it was distinctly, distinctively American.

In the late 1990s, eBay realized it needed to expand across the globe fast, if it were to move into markets before potential competitors like Yahoo sneaked in first. Its expansion plans were guided by the growth of the internet. After America, it would launch into the world's leading internet markets – Canada, Japan, Germany and the UK.

Germany was eBay's first port of call when it bought the market's largest auction site alando.de in June 1999. The German auction site had only been operating for three months before it was snapped up by eBay. It was founded by the Samwers, three savvy brothers from Cologne. One of them had spent time in Silicon Valley researching a book on start-ups, and was especially taken by eBay's business model. So it wasn't surprising that there were lots of similarities between the two companies.

Culture aside, alando.de was also a good buy for eBay because of the swift impact it had made on the German online market. Within two months of launch, it had sold over 250,000 items and had around 50,000 users. Pierre Omidyar flew out to Berlin to talk to the founders and bought the company for $42m in eBay stock.

Jim Rose, the former chairman of eBay's European competitor QXL, believes, "the smartest thing they did was buy

Alando. It was their best in-road into Europe." QXL had also tried to acquire the German start-up, but eBay got there first. Alando had a tough competitor called ricardo.de and a few years later, QXL merged with it to strengthen its European position against eBay.

It wasn't long before eBay had stamped its footprint on the new German addition. It installed a new director, who spoke flawless English and had studied at the Northwestern University's Kellogg School of Management. Legend says that he was dumbfounded when each of the six founders drew him a completely different organizational chart for the company. Within a few months, all but one of the founders had left the company.

EBay's first shout of authority, as it introduced listing fees, caused uproar among the German community. Alando had only ever asked auctioneers for a proportion of their final selling price. Alando was soon receiving over 3,000 daily emails from users protesting about the new fees. They soon acted on their disapproval and listings plunged from 1.2 million to 200,000. Then a few months later alando.de became ebay.de, and the external transformation was complete.

In the UK, eBay took a slightly different approach. The British market was already heating up to auction fever. QXL, a website launched by a *Financial Times* journalist called Tim Jackson in 1997, was building momentum. And the dominant British portals of the moment, which included Yahoo, Freeserve and AOL wanted to launch their own auction sites.

QXL was probably eBay's biggest competition across Europe. Jackson became infected with internet fever in 1996 while living in California researching a book on Intel. When he returned to the UK he was determined to be the first to introduce Europe to online auctions.

In January 1998, Quixell (QXL's original name) hosted its first online auction. Like eBay, its initial focus was computer equipment before it moved into other items. QXL's expansion across Europe was swift. It was dotcom boom time in Europe and QXL, like many other ambitious British start-ups was sprinting across the continent, staking its claim, before the American flag arrived.

In early 1999, while eBay was gazing longingly across the Atlantic, QXL was launching sites in Germany, France and Italy. It raised $12m in first round funding and recruited Jim Rose, a seasoned leader from United Information Group as chief executive officer. As eBay launched in the UK, QXL began preparing for its IPO on the London Stock Exchange and Nasdaq National Market.

Jim Rose reminisces about those heady, chaotic days with pleasure. It was a classic emerging market. In a way it was like the spice trade – the internet pioneers were all racing to jump ashore a new land first. And in the auction space, it was essential to launch and build scale as quickly as possible. "In this business it was about building a natural monopoly. Once you've got natural dominance, it becomes unassailable. So there was a race for market dominance," explains Rose.

Rose says he and his management team were not nervous about eBay launching in Europe. "We had numerous conversations but we felt they had a very US-centric view of the world. We were worried about the competition, but not about a multi-lingual platform," he reveals.

However, QXL's early business model was flawed, and this was to lead, eventually, to its defeat by eBay. In order to build momentum for its auctions, QXL had deviated away from a pure person-to-person auction business model.

It also bought inventory, which it would sell through auctions to its buyers in order to boost trade on the site. This meant its business model was a little more complicated than the lean mediating machine that was eBay. It had to concern itself with finding warehouse space to store its stock as well as create mechanisms to package and post goods to users.

With hindsight, Rose sees this as QXL's Achilles heel in the early days. "It was a mistake we made. It was all so new that we were thinking, 'Who comes first – the buyer or the seller?' We'd buy inventory to get transaction volume and then we'd shut down the business. It was not a good model because it doesn't drive economics in community trading," he admits.

EBay launched in the UK on July 4 1999, an auspicious date. Unlike its German counterpart, ebay.co.uk was being built from scratch, using an all-British staff based in the leafy London suburb of Chiswick, advised by Omidyar and the management team. But the British site already had a head start: around 10 percent of eBay's American website users were Brits.

The American site was anglicized. Categories for Muffin the Mule and Dr Who's Tardis were added, and US spellings were corrected. There were some inevitable teething problems as the American leadership of eBay grappled to get to grips with British sensibilities. For example, when eBay UK sent out the standard response to a customer complaint it was not well-received. The letter was punctuated by flocks of exclamation marks, and the more sceptical Brits said it smacked of insincerity.

Again to American eBay's surprise, the new message boards were not as resounding a success as they had been in the US. British people just weren't comfortable wittering on to strangers about this and that; about what they had for breakfast and what they were doing at the weekend. The alien concept of online chitter chatter would take some time to embed itself into the British consciousness.

In 2000, QXL continued its relentless march across Europe. The British online auctioneer expanded into Poland, Denmark, Sweden, Norway, Finland and Switzerland. It grew mainly through acquisition and a merger with the dominant German auction player ricardo.de. The company was renamed QXL Ricardo plc.

Unfortunately for QXL, eBay.co.uk and eBay.de were beginning to gain a momentum of their own. By the end of 2000, just a year after their respective launches, it looked as if eBay may have won the battle. Some reports suggest that its new German and English sites were pulling in $87m in sales compared with QXL and Ricardo's combined $38m.[64] Today, the Brits spend more time on ebay.co.uk than any other website.

The following year, in 2001, eBay began its own march across Europe acquiring the French online auctioneer iBazar. It had 2.4 million registered users and was the leading site in France, Italy, Spain, Belgium, Portugal and the Netherlands. By the end of the year, eBay was the leading online auction site in 16 of the 17 markets it operated in.

QXL Ricardo continued to fight back. It signed deals with all the major portals across Europe to become their auction partner. "Then we were all competing with eBay," recalls Rose. "They outspent us by 10 or 20:1. It won the battle market by market and we underestimated the power of the UK trading community. In hindsight, we made a mistake not getting to the pure play auction model sooner than we did."

Rose remembers interviewing consumers in France, Italy and Spain about eBay; they all had negative brand recognition of the brightly coloured American brand. And he points out that virtually all of eBay's expansion overseas was through acquisition rather than organic growth. The only successful exception is the UK market. EBay's growth strategy was very simple: it identified an auction leader in a local market, bought it and rolled out its systems and processes. EBay took an all-American approach to international growth.

JAPANESE MISTAKES

And sometimes, an all-American growth strategy can backfire, as eBay discovered to its detriment in 2002. It turned out that the American online auctioneer was not invincible after all, when it got trounced in Japan. And its competitor was not an ambitious, local start-up with a back street knowledge of cultural nuances in the market, but Yahoo Japan.

EBay's first mistake in the Japanese market was arriving late. Yahoo Japan had managed to get there first. And just five months early seemed to be long enough to sew up the market. By the time eBay arrived in the world's second largest internet market in February 2000, online auctions, courtesy of Yahoo were flying.

By summer 2001, Yahoo Japan, which was also the country's largest portal, had 95 percent of the online auction market, where $1.6bn worth of goods had been traded the previous year. In contrast, eBay Japan, which specialized in auctions and was used to ruling the roost in auction markets, had a measly 3 percent share.

Yahoo Japan had one crucial advantage. Softbank Corp owned 51 percent of the portal, and its CEO Masayoshi Son was keen for Yahoo to launch an auction site. "If auctions are not a success, that's OK. But if they are, and we're late, we'll be too late," he warned Yahoo Japan's management.[65]

EBay's overly American stance had no place in the tough Japanese market. Auctioneers were not impressed by eBay's decision to charge commission when Yahoo was free. The decision to require sellers to provide credit card numbers was also culturally unpopular; it was a hassle for the young Japanese, who don't have plastic and prefer to pay cash on delivery or via bank transfer.

EBay also took too long to embellish its Japanese sites with the local nuances and touches to appeal to users. Alterations such as adding product reviews, newsletters and horoscopes took months to be applied to the site. As Meg Whitman was repeatedly questioned about eBay's struggles she would talk of patience. "We're in it for the marathon, not the sprint."

But in February 2002, eBay was forced to concede defeat and retreat from the market. The Japanese language site was closed down. While eBay only offered 25,000 products on its site, Yahoo

Japan had nearly 3.5 million items. It was eBay's first big defeat, under the spotlight of the world stage. Later, Whitman was to describe it as the biggest strategic mistake eBay had made to date. Japan has grown to become the second-largest e-commerce market in the world.

"We didn't have the first-mover advantage in Japan. Yahoo Japan launched its auction product six to eight months before us. It was able to leverage its incredibly strong position with its portal. With 20-20 hindsight, I don't think we executed as well as we might have. In terms of the management team and support to them in the US, we were a much less experienced company in early 2000 than we are today," Whitman has said.[66]

The reason that Japan was such a big mistake for eBay was because it could have been very different. In 1999, eBay had been offered a rare opportunity by Softbank's Masayoshi Son, who wanted Yahoo to partner with eBay on a Japanese auction site. EBay's leadership rejected the deal because they didn't feel comfortable collaborating with Yahoo in Japan, while competing with the portal elsewhere.

The decision to remain independent nearly shut out the Asian market. Then, in December 2007, eBay swallowed its pride and decided to team up with Yahoo Japan to offer its US auctions to the portal's 20 million users. EBay's decision to collaborate may help the global auctioneer finally establish a foothold in Asia.

SCALING CHINESE WALLS

EBay continued to crusade in Asia. Its next battleground was China, joining the flurry of Western companies trying to drive their flag into Chinese territory. Despite fierce local competition, eBay pushed into China in 2003 hoping that it would become its biggest market in five to 10 years. MP3 players and ancient jade were especially popular items on eBay China. Other more unusual auctions have included 16 dairy cows and a table tennis match against World Champion Wang Liqin.

The fight to scale up quickly begun again. This time eBay's enemy didn't start out as Yahoo, but as a colourful, eccentric Chinese entrepreneur called Jack Ma. That was, until he sold a stake of his business alibaba.com to Yahoo for $1.7bn in 2005. His internet venture Alibaba shares an investor with Yahoo – Softbank, which helped to broker the deal between the two companies.

Jack Ma has a penchant for telling stories and creating publicity. He says he discovered the potential of the internet in 1995 when he typed the words "beer" and "China" into Yahoo's search engine. When nothing came back, he decided to create websites for Chinese companies.

In 2003, when eBay acquired China's largest online auction house eachnet.com for $180m, Ma created taobao.com ("searching for treasure" in Mandarin) to compete head to head with eBay. And the following year, when eBay moved Eachnet onto its global platform, its product listings plunged to 250,000 from 780,000.

Ma likes to get his new staff to do handstands so they could see eBay in a new way. He argued that competing with eBay seemed less daunting when you're upside down. "It may be the shark in the ocean, but we are the crocodile in the Yangtze River," he jousted.[67] To take on the decidedly American presence of eBay, Taobao emphasized its local staff and cultural roots; its online moderators take on the personae of characters in famous Chinese kung fu novels.

In 2005, eBay sunk around $100m into China and invested large numbers in marketing. Traditionally, eBay likes its community to spread the word of the service virally all by themselves; but it had learnt in Japan that this softly, softly approach doesn't always work. So in the summer of 2005, Shanghai was plastered with eBay advertising: there were eBay ads on Shanghai buses, in the streets and on the TV, and karaoke bar customers were rewarded with an hour's free singing if they registered at eBay.

EBay drew on some of its mistakes in Japan. In China, it charged auction users almost nothing to sell items of set-up online stores. But eBay struggled to compete with Alibaba's Taobao auction site, which claimed more active users than eBay and pledged to stay free of charge until 2008 to help accelerate China's e-commerce development.

So far, not one Western website has succeeded in China – all the top sites are home grown. And in December 2006, eBay was forced to concede defeat and withdraw, giving control of its main China operation to Beijing-based portal and telecom service operator Tom Online. It now has a minority stake in the new joint venture.

It was a dramatic turnaround and a stark illustration of the difficulties facing foreign internet companies in China. Just one year previously in 2005, eBay's chief executive Meg Whitman had said that its $100m investment was a "sign of an unmistakeable commitment and an unstoppable determination to be number one in China." This commitment had been made clear in the same year when Whitman herself spent a long, stifling summer in Shanghai trying to shore up the business. Despite this, eBay dramatically failed to understand the Chinese market and was out-thought by its local competition.

EBAY'S SHOPPING SPREE

Following its acquisitions of two very different companies – PayPal, an online payment system, and Skype, an internet telephony start-up – eBay is morphing into a new kind of business. EBay's leaders must manage three different businesses at very different stages in their lifecycles.

And Whitman always insisted that eBay's business definition

pulls PayPal and Skype together and makes sense of the three of them. "What we do in eBay is connect buyers and sellers better than anyone else in the world. The common thread is connecting buyers and sellers," she has explained.[68]

In a more revealing interview with the *Financial Times*, Niklas Zennstrom, founder of Skype downplayed the connections between the three businesses. "We have a road map, PayPal have their road map and eBay marketplaces have their road map. If we would focus everything about synergies, we would not focus on end user experience."

In the early days, eBay had a tendency of buying businesses it thought might become competition, or that its competition might buy instead. In 2000, it bought a fixed-price online marketplace called half.com for $340m. While eBay wanted to extend its platform into fixed price sales, it was also petrified that Amazon might buy half.com instead, which would have propelled the etailer's growth from e-commerce into a virtual network. The acquisition has enabled eBay to develop its fixed-price model, with many auctions advertising a "buy-it-now" option. So, too, has eBay Express, launched in the US in Spring 2006 as a shopping site that enables users to buy products immediately at a fixed price.

EBay has also acquired stakes in a number of different businesses. They include shopping.com, a price comparison site, and online classified companies such as Kijiji and Craigslist.

If acquisitions have helped eBay diversify, so too has a new type of customer. There is a vibrant B2B marketplace thriving on eBay, where many companies sell and buy inventory. Over 40 percent of computers traded on eBay are bought for business.

"Non-users had no idea they could buy anything for business, they thought eBay was all about Beanie Babies or Barbies. But business buying is growing faster than the consumer side," says Jay Fiore, who grew the B2B side of eBay's marketplace from 2002.

PAYPAL SUCKS?

PayPal began its life in 1999 as a money transfer system that worked from palm pilot to palm pilot. Soon its founders Max Levchin and Peter Thiel realized their application would have more relevance if it worked from computer to computer, using email. At the end of the year, by offering their service for free, and using VC funds to hand out five dollars to everyone who signed up, PayPal had 12,000 registered users.

Payment had always been the weakest link in eBay's chain. While the rest of the auction could gallop along effortlessly online, transferring funds between the buyer and seller caused the process to crawl to a stop as sellers waited for a cheque or bank transfer to clear. And it wasn't long before some eBay sellers got in contact wanting to use PayPal in their auction listings. By April 2000, PayPal's 12,000 users had skyrocketed to over one million.[69]

EBay's management knew that a robust online payment system was vital for its growth, but it wasn't a business it wanted to launch itself. Online payments were a step too far from eBay's competency. Not only that, it had some understandable concerns about fraud. In 2000, PayPal was targeted by Russian and Nigerian internet crime rings and was struck with $8.9m in charge-backs for unauthorized credit card use. EBay, a public company, did not want to be hit by a similar scandal.

In April 1999, eBay acquired a small, online payment start-up called Billpoint. Unfortunately, the new company struggled to get its system up and working. By the time it was finally ready to launch on eBay in 2000, PayPal had gathered serious momentum. However, although PayPal was a popular option for eBay sellers, it was Billpoint that was the one-click way to list an item on eBay; renamed eBay Payments, its integration with eBay seemed complete.

In 2002, though, eBay had to concede defeat; by then, PayPal was handling the payments of around one in four winning auctions. EBay knew it needed to boost the use of electronic payments for auctions, so it made more sense to buy its rival than beat it. In August 2002, eBay acquired PayPal in a deal worth $1.5bn.

Today, Whitman jokes about how some critics vilified her as a crazy woman for spending so much money on a "stupid, little company." But she believes that eBay was able to unlock PayPal and enable each business to grow on its own. PayPal has grown dramatically under eBay's ownership to offer transaction services for many retailers including Harrods department store.

However, the PayPal acquisition was not entirely popular with eBay's community. Many eBayers were unhappy about the increased control eBay now had over their financial affairs. Others hated PayPal, which in its short lifespan had developed a poor reputation for customer service.

Even today, most eBay customers have a love/hate relationship with PayPal. It is not a popular brand. And it probably taints many customers' opinions of eBay. Some eBayers refuse to use PayPal and reminisce about Billpoint. Others engage themselves in long, drawn out battles with the online payment system.

At eBay University, it is always the PayPal sessions that lead to the angriest exchanges between panel and audience. Although the acquisition fitted eBay's business model, it probably damages eBay's brand. Perhaps that's one reason why eBay's leadership decided not to rename it eBay Payments.

There's a very popular website called PayPal Sucks. In 2005, it was named by *Forbes* as one of the top 10 corporate hate websites. It includes tales of database mix ups that charge accounts too often and of the freezing of powersellers' accounts if buyers have paid by stolen credit cards.

PayPal, when it works, may make transactions smoother on eBay, but it's not popular. Sellers in Australia are upset that buyers will soon only be able to use PayPal for purchases, a move that may be duplicated in bigger markets.

THE ESTONIAN CONNECTION

Skype was a different sort of acquisition for eBay. It was incredibly popular among most of its users, but some analysts were concerned by the high price eBay was prepared to pay. In September 2005, the online auction house paid a staggering $3bn for the young, European company. The stock market was unimpressed by the high price and eBay's stock plunged 7 percent when merger rumours emerged.

The price didn't seem right, but the philosophy behind the deal does. Skype is undoubtedly eBaysian. Like eBay in its early days, it grew virally as news of its free internet telephony service spread across the globe.

"We loved the Skype viral effect ... it looked a lot like eBay. It was very clear to me that something quite unique was going on at Skype – it was pioneering a whole new technology, but building a thriving ecosystem of users, developers, hardware manufacturers, chipset manufacturers," Whitman has explained.[70]

Skype was founded in 2002 by Niklas Zennstrom and Janus Friis. The Scandinavian entrepreneurs made their names creating Kazaa – in its time, the best way to steal music on the internet. This time around, the enterprising duo built Skype using Estonian technical whizzes, choosing tiny tax-haven Luxembourg as their base. Their internet telephony service enables PC users to make free telephone calls.

Skype's value lay in the 53 million customers signed up to its service. It was attracting 30,000 new users a day through word of mouth in May 2005, and 70,000 a day six months later in November 2005. But the young business was only making around $50m in revenues. While most of its services are free, the company charges for calls to mobile phones and landlines.

Rather than spend millions of dollars on marketing, the 70-employee company relies entirely on recommendation. Skype has grown virally because it's based on free communications.

Users want to tell their friends around the globe about it, so they can speak to them for free. But what will eBay use Skype for? Internet telephony becomes another channel to connect buyers and sellers.

"It had some really nice synergies with eBay and PayPal. In the case of eBay, there is communication synergy. And with PayPal, this whole notion of actually PayPal being the wallet on Skype, and every new Skype user getting a PayPal account and vice versa," Whitman has said.[71]

While the cultural and communication fit between Skype and eBay makes sense, there is concern among some analysts that eBay won't be able to make money out of Skype to justify its price. One telecoms analyst joked that if he were the owner of Skype and someone had offered $3bn, he would take the money and run. And in 2007, eBay had to take a $1.4bn write-down for its Skype purchase.

Patti Freeman Evans, senior analyst, retail at Jupiter Research says that Skype is consistent with eBay's model of putting buyers and sellers together. But was it expensive? "It seems like a lot of money to me!" she admits.

Skype certainly adds a communication function onto eBay, but what else can it offer? Analysts have suggested that Skype could also add telephone bidding to eBay or use some of its file transfer technology to sell online content such as music or videos. Whitman laughed when asked about eBay's ability to monetize the deal. "Well I certainly hope we're gonna be able to monetize it!" she retorted.

In April 2008, John Donahoe just one month into the job as eBay's CEO gave a strong hint that he was considering scrapping the ill-starred acquisition. "If the synergies are strong, we'll keep it in our portfolio. If not, we'll reassess it," he told the *Financial Times*.[72]

A TRIANGULAR-SHAPED BUSINESS

And over a decade since its launch, eBay has evolved from its roots as an American online flea market. No longer reliant on the auction format, it also deals in e-commerce. No longer reliant on Beanie Baby collectors, it also deals with large corporations. EBay Express enables buyers to purchase items for a fixed-price, just like they would on Amazon, alongside acquisitions such as shopping.com. Meanwhile, online classified acquisitions like Craigslist and Kijiji are enabling eBay to dabble in the online advertising market.

And then, of course, there's eBay, the telephony expert through Skype, and eBay the payment merchant, through PayPal. So what should eBay be known for today? Whitman says that eBay owns three of the top five brands on the internet. "We have the number one e-commerce for franchise, the number one online payment standard and the number one voice communications player in the world," she boasts.[73]

Some critics suggest that eBay's metamorphosis from auction to fixed price, from personal to corporate, is evidence that it is thrashing around to find growth. They say that its market has reached saturation and that eBay will lose relevance over the next 15 years.

But, for now, at least, eBay is a triangular-shaped business with three brands to nurture – eBay, PayPal and Skype. It's a future that Omidyar and Skoll would have struggled to predict 10 years ago, as they grappled with the organic growth of a vibrant auctioning community.

Chapter 9

The Heart of Darkness

> "We live as we dream – alone."
> **Joseph Conrad**

EBay has a dark side. It's not all shooting stars, perfect markets, empowered traders and excitable shoppers greeting the postman. There is a murky eBay world lurking beneath the surface. It is a world of fakes and scams and fraud; a world of rip offs, body parts, pornography and pirate DVDs. It's a place that the official side of eBay tries to distance itself from, but it's never far away.

It's eBay's black market. It's like the rooms behind the stalls at a souk in any street in any city across the world. While the market trader might appear to be selling carpets and perfume on the outside, the right whispered word to the right person can take you into a shrouded, smoky room and a hidden world.

It reminds me of the scorching, desert city in the Star Wars films Mos Espa, where impoverished settlers scratch a living from gambling and trading on the black market. There's nothing wrong with eBay having a smell of the Wild West about it, all the best real-life bazaars do. But some elements of eBay's bandit country are darker than they should be.

It isn't the picture of eBay most people are used to seeing. EBay is a remarkable dotcom story; it's a heartening tale of how strangers learning to trust one another can build a marketplace together. But inevitably, eBay's fundamental belief that people are basically good makes it vulnerable to shifty opportunists, fraudsters, scam artists and criminals.

ALL HUMAN LIFE IS HERE

It is probably inevitable that the mad, mad souk of eBay sells the most bizarre items. Wares that have been peddled on the online auction site include a man's virginity, a human kidney, a human testicle, a baby, 200 pounds of cocaine and a soul. Before eBay banned the selling of guns and ammunition in 1999, peddlers traded a rocket launcher, a missile and a bazooka.

THE MAN WHO PLACED HIS SOUL ON THE AUCTION BLOCK

For sale: The chance to save my soul

February 3 2004

41 bids

Winning bid: $504

For each $10 of the final bid, I will attend an hour of church services. I'm an atheist, but I suspect I have been missing out on something. Perhaps being around a group of people who will show me 'the way' could do what no one else has done before. This is possibly the best chance anyone has of changing me.

You can even buy a pound of flesh on eBay. It's surprisingly easy to buy human remains at the online auction house. A scientist blogs excitedly about buying a human femur with an attached artificial knee joint on eBay, complete with gouge marks where someone slipped with a power tool.

THE MAN WHO TRIED TO SELL VITAL ORGANS ON EBAY

For sale: One fully functional kidney

September 1 1999

Bidding began at $25,000

Winning bid: $5.7m, before eBay closed auction

You can choose either kidney. Buyer pays all transplant and medical costs. Of course only one for sale, as I need the other one to live. Serious bids only.

In 1999, someone calling themselves "hchero" tried to sell a kidney on eBay. The ad for the fully functional kidney read: "You can choose either kidney. Buyer pays all transplant and medical costs. Of course only one for sale, as I need the other one to live. Serious bids only." The bid went as high as $5.7m before eBay intervened and closed the auction down.

In 2003, a 49-year-old British father called Peter Randall tried to sell his kidney on eBay to raise money for special therapy for his six-year-old daughter, who suffers from cerebral palsy. He set a reserve price of $85,000, but the ad was removed by eBay after a week. Media publicity meant, however, that Randall went on to raise over £60,000 ($113,696). (In a bizarre, tabloid-esque twist, Randall later abandoned his wife and sick daughter for a 23-year-old Thai bride.)

In January 2004, Rose Reid, 18, from London, decided to sell her virginity on eBay to pay off her student debts. The Bristol University student said she'd rather sleep with a stranger than face years of poverty. She received more than 400 offers within three days, including one of £10,000 ($18,950.) While eBay halted the auction, Rosie continued the auction on her own website. Fortunately, it was bought by a businessman who agreed to give her the money without taking the "service."

THE FEMALE STUDENT WHO TRIED TO SELL HER VIRGINITY

For sale: Young woman's virginity

January 2004

400 bids

Winning bid: Reached £10,000 before eBay closed auction. (Student, Rosie Reid continued the auction on her own website.)

Eighteen-year-old university student looking to sell virginity. Never lost it due to lesbianism. Will bung in free massage if you are any good. Picture on request.

Some auctions are more macabre. In 2004, a 35-year-old German mother and her 41-year-old boyfriend were investigated by local police for attempted human trafficking when they tried to sell the woman's eight-year-old daughter on eBay. They wrote: "You can play with her, or sell her to gypsies. She's a real working toy." The couple claimed the auction was a joke.

Similarly, in 2005, on eBay's Chinese website eachnet, babies from the rural Henan province were offered for sale. Boys were advertised for 28,000 yuan ($3,450), while girls were offered for 13,000 yuan ($1,603). The seller under the user name "Chuangxinzhe Yongyuan" or "innovator forever" said the babies would be available within 100 days of their birth and would benefit China's millions of infertile couples.

EBay always cancels the auctions of illegal items, if it can spot them. But it relies on its community to highlight problem auctions. And it's difficult to say whether these macabre auctions are hoaxes or not; some are and some aren't. These sales have become folklore. Today, a search for "virginity" on eBay only reveals novelty badges and T-shirts that proudly proclaim: "I sold my virginity on eBay."

THE MAN WHO SOLD A GHOST IN A JAR

For sale: Ghost in a jar

June 6 2003

84 bids

Winning bid: $90 million, but many bids were fake

Back in the early 1980's, I came across an old abandoned cemetery. After digging down about 2 feet my shovel struck a wooden box that had nearly rotted out. There were 2 jars and an old journal in the box. The jars had some strange writing and symbols on them.

While getting the jars out of the ground, I dropped one and it broke. A black mist or something seeped out of it. That night, I had my first visit from what I can only describe as "The Black Thing". Therefore, I am offering to you, if you dare, the "Ghost in the Jar". Be advised that once you buy this it is yours and I will have nothing ever again to do with it! ALL SALES ARE FINAL! I WILL NOT BE HELD RESPONSIBLE FOR ANYTHING THAT HAPPENS ONCE THE TRANSACTION IS COMPLETE!

THE FAKE FACTOR

Every buyer on eBay has the will to believe. That means they want to believe that they're buying something special and authentic on eBay. They want to believe that their fellow eBayer is a good, honest person. And they want to believe that maybe, just maybe, they're buying a valuable treasure. And it is this "will to believe" that enables fraudsters to peddle fake items on eBay successfully.

In 1998, a bored lawyer called Kenneth Walton tried to sell a fake painting on eBay. He doctored a brightly coloured abstract painting that he bought from a junk shop for $8 with the signature "RD52." The RD stood for Richard Diebenkorn, an obscure 20th century Californian artist. Within a few days, the fake was attracting bids of over $100,000.

It was not the first fake painting Walton had sold on eBay. He had honed his technique and accompanied his sales with appropriately folksy blurb to convince bidders that he was a clueless seller who didn't realize the value of the treasure he was selling. He told them the painting was kept in his garage because his wife wouldn't let him keep it in the house. (Walton didn't have a wife or a house.) And he didn't place a reserve price on the auction.

Walton also used multiple online identities to anonymously boost bidding, an illegal practice known as "shill bidding." His partner in crime Ken Fetterman would also place bids on the auction to boost the final sale price. It didn't take long for the FBI to come knocking on his door. The six-figure bids on the auction had attracted the attention of art expects who suspected a fraud. Meanwhile, eBay suspended the auction and froze Walton's accounts; he was charged with shill bidding and put on probation.

Walton believes that his case was used as an example by eBay. Once the FBI got involved, eBay wanted to quash the site's reputation as a haven for fraud. They wanted to send the message that there were big penalties for breaking eBay's rules. The old system of eBay issuing warning after warning to rule-breaking eBayers before suspending their account was not always effective. Today, eBay says it has over 2,000 people continually monitoring the site to prevent fraud.

But buyers will still often cling to the thought that they might have discovered a secret treasure. The winning bidder of the fake Diebenkorn was livid when the auction was suspended. He wanted to cling to the belief that he might have bought a masterpiece; he threatened Walton with legal action when the sale was cancelled.

"There's this optimistic self-delusion. It's really big in the art world. People really want to believe they have found something good. I've been there. I've bought things that weren't real, that I've taken a chance on," Walton has said.[74]

And that's part of the problem for eBay. However strict it becomes, however frequently it involves external investigators such as the FBI, fraud will always be perpetuated by the seductive thrill of the auction. Walton recalls the huge adrenalin rush of selling bad art for good money, while for the buyers, there's always that sneaking hope that they've stumbled upon something precious.

And it's not just fake art: fake designer brands from handbags to jewellery inevitably play a starring role on eBay. The anonymity and reach of the internet makes it perfect for selling knockoffs. And eBay, as the biggest online marketplace, has become the centre of a new universe of fakery.

Today, dealers of fake goods are far more likely to be sophisticated internet traders than market boys flogging their wares from the back of a van. The global fashion counterfeit industry has grown into a £306bn ($576bn) industry. Some estimates suggest that counterfeiting accounts for up to 7 percent of all world trade.

And while it's easy to argue that selling or buying a fake Louis Vuitton handbag never harmed anybody, it's not so easy to prove. International investigators such as Interpol believe that counterfeiters' profits are used to fund life-threatening criminal activity, albeit at several steps removed.

While the products themselves aren't going to kill anyone, the profits from selling them are financing terrorism and are used for money laundering, according to authorities. In Europe, the biggest business in counterfeiting is among active terrorist groups in Italy and Northern Ireland.[75]

Often the best way of spotting a fake is when the sale price seems too good to be true. Real boutique designer brands cost in excess of £500; they're not likely to sell for less than £50. One expert in identifying Louis Vuitton fakes has estimated that of every 100 Louis Vuitton items for sale on eBay, fewer than eight are genuine.[76]

In 2004, Zena Bailey, a 31-year-old British fashion follower spotted a rare Louis Vuitton cherry blossom papillon bag on eBay. It looked like a genuine, limited edition bag that is normally only available for VIPs and has a huge waiting list. Bidding begun at £350 and after a few days it was just Bailey and an American buyer called "Traci Lacey" competing for the bag. Bailey secured the bag for £960.

But when the bag arrived, Bailey realized it was a fake. The screws securing the bag looked cheap, the leather seemed grainy and the colour wasn't quite right. She went to the police and in

June 2005, the bag's seller Angela Makki was found guilty of selling fake goods and given a six-month suspended sentence.

It's not just the duped buyers that feel aggrieved at fakes on eBay; the brand owners are not happy either. In July 2008, a French court ordered eBay to pay 38.8m euros in damages to LVMH, a luxury-goods company, for letting fake versions of its designer bags to be sold. In the US, Tiffany, the jewellery brand, is suing eBay for facilitating the trade of counterfeit Tiffany items. It's almost impossible for the company to police a site that has over 250 million members and 60 million items for sale at any one time.

EBay says that just 0.01 percent of transactions are confirmed as illegal, which means that just 6,000 items at any one time across the global marketplace are fraudulent. But this estimate is only confirmed cases, and critics suggest that fraud goes well beyond eBay's official numbers. After all, fraudulent or not, eBay is still benefiting financially from the auctions. EBay makes a lot of money from a lot of small, unhappy transactions that will probably never be traced or identified.

THE EMPEROR'S NEW CLOTHES

Some of eBay's most audacious examples of fraud occur when buyers bid, win and pay for non-existent items. There are auctions for empty boxes, non-existent lap tops and digital cameras and thin air. While the money flutters its way towards the criminal sellers, there's no item being posted in return. EBay is hosting hundreds of auctions for the emperor's new clothes.

Twenty-three-year-old Michael Paul Jackson, now in prison in North Carolina in the US, still marvels at how easy it was to post fake auctions on eBay. He managed to sell products he didn't own for over four years, stealing over $120,000 from 100 eBay users. "I never knew how easy it was to manipulate people. It was like taking candy from a baby," he has said.[77]

Jackson would raid photos of laptops and digital cameras

from other people's auctions and pretend that he owned the items. He would often offer a killer deal that bargain hunters found impossible to resist. Then he'd receive a fat cheque or postal order from the winner, but would not post the item, because he never had it in the first place. Jackson was having the time of his life, buying his girlfriend diamond jewellery and popping over to Europe on holiday.

The inherent trust in strangers that the eBay business model requires means it's surprisingly easy for con artists to sell items that don't exist or dupe buyers into paying lots of money for an empty box. Teresa Smith, a 26-year-old from Massachusetts, was able to collect over $855,000 from 330 people, before turning herself in. "Teresa's a very good talker," explained one duped buyer.[78] On eBay, everyone dreams of being an easy winner. But the only guaranteed winner in any auction is eBay itself.

FLAWS IN THE SYSTEM

So how do fraudsters manipulate eBay's regulations? While the feedback system is not watertight, when it works it should enable the eBay community to police and regulate themselves, and alienate those who abuse the fundamental trust of the organization.

In March 2000, eBay management made some tweaks to the feedback system, which they hoped would eliminate instances of abuse. From then on, feedback was restricted to transactions only: buyers and sellers rating each other on specific auctions. Previously, feedback had been a free-for-all, with eBayers commending fellow members for being particularly helpful on the message boards, but also occasionally lambasting another member with negative feedback following a bad experience.

However, the feedback ratings remained a flawed system. Buyers who suffered bad experiences often kept quiet for fear the seller would retaliate with negative feedback about them. I once received a dirty, smelly jumper that was certainly not new as implied in the listing. But I took no action. I left no feedback because it would have been negative and I didn't want to receive the same in return; after all, I was gunning for my first star.

And the fascinating thing about feedback is that it doesn't tell you about the person, but about how good an eBayer they are. They might be horrid in real life but be draped in shooting stars in eBay's parallel universe.

All eBayers fall under the spell of the feedback system. It feels like the most important thing in the world to maintain a clean balance sheet. Most savvy eBay sellers wouldn't leave feedback for a buyer until they'd received feedback themselves. EBay can thus present a false picture of the "relationship" between buyer and seller.

There are people who buy and sell user IDs, and also members with multiple IDs. Some shifty opportunists hop from user ID to user ID, feeding the system with fake information and stolen credit cards so eBay can't track who they are. They buy their own item using multiple IDs and give themselves glowing feedback. I've spoken to many sellers who opened up another account using another credit card when their eBay account was suspended. They lose their feedback, but professional sellers can soon build up their ratings again.

In 2007, eBay tweaked the system again launching Feedback 2.0, which allows buyers to anonymously rate sellers in more detail on item description, communication, shipping time and handling charges. In January 2008, eBay announced sellers would no longer be able to leave negative or neutral feedback for buyers, in an attempt to encourage buyers to leave honest feedback without fearing retaliation.

In a renewed effort to weed out unreliable traders, sellers with a low rating will find their goods fall to the bottom of a product search, and weaker sellers will be forced to use a guaranteed payment system like PayPal. Sellers were up in arms at the changes and organized a global boycott of the site on May 1 2008.

EBAY'S QUANDARY

It is eBay's hands-off business model that makes it vulnerable to fraud. It's not so much an auction house as a meeting place and eBay purposefully doesn't watch everything that happens. It hasn't got the time, and it doesn't want to. It doesn't want to know, it doesn't want to get involved. And eBay's lack of involvement, the fact it is unburdened by armies of customer service people, shipping facilities or hangar-size warehouses, is one of the reasons it's such a profit machine.

But fraud is bad news for eBay. It means members of the community lose faith in eBay, when the online auctioneer needs a level of trust in order to operate. Already, there is a number of disgruntled victim groups noisily spreading their horror stories of fraud on eBay all over the internet. At some point soon, if it hasn't already, fraud will affect eBay's reputation.

"On a scale of one to 10, I'd give eBay a two for dealing with fraud. I got nothing from eBay – no support, nothing. I couldn't even submit a fraud claim because it was past the allotted time to file," said one victim. She hasn't used eBay since she was conned out of $1,400 in 2002.[79]

It's a difficult dilemma for eBay. On the one hand, the online auctioneer wants to stamp out fraud. However, the more vocal and active it becomes about fraud the more vulnerable it may become to legal action. So far, its status as a passive provider of a marketplace has shielded it from legal responsibility.

THE WITNESS

EBay's status as witness rather than responsible party was established in 1998 by employee number 36. Brad Handler was hired as the online auctioneer's first lawyer at the end of 1997. He immediately realized how critical it was for eBay's long-term success to establish the principle that it was only a venue and therefore not responsible for items for sale on its site. If eBay could successfully argue that it was similar to a newspaper classified section, then all would be well; but if it was regarded more like a store then it could be held responsible.

Around the same time, eBay established that while it would be prepared to pull down illegal auctions, it could not actively vet the millions of auctions in advance. Instead, it was up to brand owners and fellow auctioneers to inform eBay management of any instances of fraud.

However, eBay has been gradually getting more and more involved with the thorny issue of fraud. As early as January 1999, following a spate of scandals including fake, oddly-coloured Furbies, eBay unveiled its first anti-fraud campaign. It said it would suspend non-paying bidders for 30 days after one warning and bar shill bidders for 30 days after their first offence and permanently after their second.

Since then, eBay has steadily increased its investment in fraud prevention. Its anti-fraud operation used to consist of three people in customer services; now it is a dedicated division that includes lawyers and investigators. And Meg Whitman insists that fraud is an issue that concerns her: "I worry about it, I focus on it, I think about it a lot."[80] She says that she was determined to become more proactive following a discussion with board member Howard Schultz (founder of Starbucks) who told her: "Meg, it's about the character of the company."[81]

AN INVOLVED COMMUNITY

It's not only eBay management that are concerned about how fraud might damage the reputation of the online auctioneer. The most valuable members of eBay's community, its powersellers, are also worried that their businesses may be affected by bad press about eBay's underworld.

In the UK, a collection of well-respected powersellers has formed a trade body called FOEB, the Federation of eBay Businesses. Working alongside the online auctioneer, the FOEB is trying to promote the positive aspects of trading on eBay. Many members currently believe there is too much negative press about fraud and scams and illegal activity, which could deter new members from joining.

Most powersellers have been untouched by fraud and remain the shining-eyed evangelists of eBay's business model. For them, the community of strangers who can trust one another is the unshakeable foundation of their businesses. While fraud may happen, they believe it normally catches out the naïve ones, who would have been duped elsewhere at some point.

Chris, a British powerseller is not sympathetic towards eBay's victims of fraud. While he's still miffed about a couple of bounced cheques, he says it's not bad considering how large his turnover is. "Some people are daft. There are people on eBay who should never be in business; they expect to be spoon fed. I can't understand why people don't budget for fraud," he says.

He's also shocked by the gullibility of some of the buyers who become victims of eBay con artists. "They wouldn't send cash by Western Union to an unknown seller if they spotted something in the Yellow Pages, they might send a deposit instead. Some people who see a deal that's too good to believe, throw all common sense out of the window," he concludes.

And it's true, and once more it comes back to the inherent problem of "the will to believe." All buyers, and sellers on eBay want to see the best in people, and they want to believe that they have stumbled on a very special bargain. And that's why eBay will always struggle to contain fraud. The excitement of the environment and the thrill of the auction almost encourage it, as everyone looks for those deals that are too good to be true.

A QUESTION OF RESPONSIBILITY

However, eBay's determination to distance itself as much as possible from the naughty antics of its community is not good text book corporate behaviour. EBay's murky underworld is the most urgent corporate social responsibility issue for the business.

While other companies in other industries must grapple with CSR issues such as child labour, transparent supply chains, environmental policies and fat-cat pay packets, eBay needs to control something arguably more fundamental: illegal and unethical trade. The empty boxes, the human remains, the young girl's virginity, the fake painting, the fake handbag, the pirate DVDs and the empty promises – all these could become too big a part of the eBay brand identity.

The eBay brand with all its wholesome ideals and beliefs in the fundamental good in people will be damaged if it is dragged into a murky underworld. More than any other brand, trust is the cornerstone of eBay. After all, without trust, why else would so many perfect strangers begin trading with one another across the world?

Chapter 10

The eBay Effect

> "I've got a message from the US Post Office. EBAY WE LOVE YOU!"
> **Jack Potter, head of the US Postal Service**

EBay stretches beyond the boundaries of its vast online bartering kingdom. Its influence has also seeped into society and culture. The eBay effect has made its mark on shopping habits, trading behaviour and attitudes to consuming. The online auctioneer has reinvigorated the age of collecting and taught traditional brands the importance of involving and empowering communities and individuals.

Welcome to the eBay effect. A cultural movement whose influence pervades so many different aspects of society from shopping to employment and friendship. A phenomenon that enables a sole trader in Guatemala to sell their wares to the urban metropolis in Europe and shines a global spotlight on a toasted cheese sandwich that resembles the Virgin Mary.

LIVING IN EBAY'S SUBURBS

Like all phenomena, eBay has spawned a crop of businesses on its periphery. These are the entrepreneurial companies that are benefiting from the eBay effect. They oil the cogs and wheels of the budding online auctioneers and make a tidy profit in the process. Without eBay, they probably wouldn't exist.

Drop-off stores are some of the most interesting new businesses to crop up on the periphery of eBay. They would arguably not exist if it weren't for the eBay effect. Created to serve all those busy individuals who would love to sell and profit from eBay, if only they had the time, drop-off stores tried to cater for a valuable niche. The demise of Auctioning4u in the UK suggests the economics of the business model didn't quite add up.

been oiled by middlemen like dealers and agents, the internet makes them more redundant. It means it's easier, and therefore economically efficient, for an individual to control their own transactions. It's no longer important to have a cosy antiques shop on a quaint high street; anyone who sells anything on eBay immediately has a retail market of millions at their fingertips.

A QUESTION OF CHARITY

Thanks to the eBay effect, charity is most likely to begin and end at home. It's yet another example of how eBay has influenced broader, societal trends and changed the way we dispose of unwanted goods. It has taught the masses that one person's rubbish is another one's treasure.

Charity shops are losing thousands of pounds a week as people opt to sell their unwanted possessions on eBay rather than give them away. One report suggested medium-sized charities are facing losses of up to £50,000 a year – often as much as a 10th of the revenue from charity shops. Charities have also reported a 5 percent drop in high-quality donations, such as designer clothes.[85]

The problem for charity shops, then, is not only that fewer people are donating unwanted possessions but also that their donations are declining in value. In 2005, nearly half of 98 charities quizzed cited eBay as one of the major threats to their custom.[86]

Some charity shops, however, are attempting to battle eBay's growing influence by using it as a sales channel themselves. Oxfam is selling more valuable items at the online auction, rather than through its bricks-and-mortar outlets. Shop managers are slowly being trained to split donations into items that can be sold on the high street and collectors' items that are shipped to a special eBay shop in Leeds. EBay items now generate around £0,000 a year for the charity and over 100 of Oxfam's 800 shops

It's a business model that takes the hassle out of using eBay. While some people love the all-consuming nature of online auctions – the listing, the packing, the posting – others just don't have the time, or the inclination. In the US, there are over 7,000 outlets offering this service to eBay users, including AuctionDrop and QuikDrop.

Then, there are the technology companies, businesses that flog software to eBayers to help them buy and sell goods more effectively. There's the sniping software packages that enable bidders to win an auction at the last minute, as well as special programming software that helps eBay traders list, sell and track their items more effectively. There's even software to help entrepreneurs run their accounts.

And obviously, they're all for sale on eBay. Everything a bidding auctioneer might need to run their business can be bought in the marketplace. There's bubble wrap, cardboard boxes and masking tape from companies like Andrew Dudley's Postalsupplies. There's "how to guides" about how to make a fortune on eBay, there's lessons from powersellers and a web template for listings. There's even an auction entitled, "I will help you make money on eBay the legal way" that guarantees 100 percent satisfaction.

IT'S A HARSH, HARSH WORLD

While many eBay-related businesses continually appear on the sidelines, there are those that disappear into thin air. The eBay effect may have created opportunities for some entrepreneurs but it doesn't protect them from the harsh cycle of business. EBay's community boards occasionally have strands where users try to track down traders who've disappeared. They sound concerned, upset. It's like the shop next door closing down in the middle of the night, and not being able to say goodbye.

Sometimes, even eBay celebrities melt away into thin air. John

Hannon, better known as parrothead88, used to sell postage supplies to the eBay community. Based in Florida, he exploded onto eBay's public arena when he became the first trader to reach the heady heights of a 10,000 feedback rating and earn a shooting star at the end of 2001.

Today, the powerseller who made eBay history is nowhere to be found. With a heady feedback score of 74,499, he is no longer registered on eBay. Poignantly for Hannon, his last page of transactions is full of negative feedback. In May 2006, online forums across the world were buzzing with speculation about where eBay's historical powerseller might be.

THE POSTMAN KNOCKS TWICE

And it's not just new businesses that have benefited from the eBay effect. National Post Offices across the world must have breathed a sigh of relief as eBay pervaded the world's consciousness. Until eBay came along, it seemed as if technology and the internet might sound the death-knell for old-fashioned snail mail.

In a British newspaper survey of 100 post offices, 76 identified regular eBay sellers as a source of their rise in custom, and 67 said that over half the parcels sent from their branch came from eBay. Nearly 70 percent of the post offices had earned an additional £1,000 to £3,000 a week from eBay sellers.[82]

Today, everyone has had the tedious experience of queuing behind an eBayer posting scores of parcels from the Post Office. Powersellers talk fondly of the relationship they've nurtured with their local postmaster. It's like a business friendship from bygone days – they're made cups of tea, and the post room workers worry something might be wrong if they don't see them.

EBay sellers recognize other eBay traders while they're at the local post office. "There's like half a dozen of us with big piles of boxes and stuff, and we all look at each other out of the corner of our eye," says Alan, a self-employed eBayer.[83]

And the Post Office is thrilled. During eBay Live! in 2006, Jack Potter, the head of the US Postal Service, made a speech after Meg Whitman's contribution. She introduced his company as the "unsung hero" of eBay. Meanwhile, buzzing from the adulation that lingered from Whitman's exit, he shouted: "I've got a message from the US Post Office: We love you!"

DUSTY, OLD ANTIQUES

There are winners and losers on the periphery of every phenomenon, and inevitably some businesses are suffering because of the eBay effect. A British antique dealer called Douglas Young believes that eBay will cause the death of all antique and collectible shops. In the past few years, the turnover of his antique shop on the British coast has fallen by 70–75 percent, something he blames solely on eBay.

EBay means increased competition – an alternative market place for antiques and collectibles – and it means increas consumer "literacy." People are much savvier about the poten value of their goods than they used to be.

"Someone came into my shop wanting to sell me a p watch and we agreed on a price of £200. But the next day, visited his house to give him the money and collect the watch, he'd changed his mind. He said he wanted no l £450 because he'd just seen a pocket watch sell for that on eBay," recalls Young.[84]

In eBay world, it's the middle men like antique de are getting squeezed out of the supply chain. While so are learning to sell their wares online, it's becoming hard for them to find goods and sell them on at a wants to sell their grandmother's heirlooms to an a if they can do it themselves on eBay?

The reason for the decline of antique deale Young is simple economics. While commerce sell on the global marketplace. Other savvy charities are exploiting eBay as a marketing channel for auctioning celebrity donations.

Taking money from charities is not good publicity for eBay. Who wants to be known as the company that makes its money by encouraging people to line their own pockets rather than give things to good causes? The need to avert a brand reputation disaster is probably one reason why eBay is trying to actively help charities boost their fortunes online. It's certainly a favourite topic of eBay's management.

In 2006, the company launched an initiative called eBay for Charity to help charities make more money through eBay. So far, over 800 charities have signed up in the UK. It provides consultancy to registered charities wanting to sell items through eBay and also donates a percentage of its own cut of the final fee. (If 100 percent is being donated to charity, then eBay will waive its fee.) It has also created a mechanism to enable sellers to donate part of their proceeds to an eBay registered charity.

Just as retailers are learning to use eBay as a way of selling unwanted stock, so charity shops need to evolve their business model for the 21st century. With one hand eBay takes some of their revenue away; with the other it extends the offer of help.

EBAY'S CRYSTAL BALL

Life is not as simple for eBay as it used to be. In fact, it's quite complicated. Meg Whitman liked to talk about eBay's mushrooming growth in terms of town and country planning. "Think of what happens when a small community becomes a big city," she has said on more than one occasion.[87]

And if anything, eBay's growth is one of its worst enemies. How can it stay small, while being big? How can it maintain its unique sense of community when its community is the same size as the fifth largest country in the world? And how can eBay protect the best interests of its population when it needs to keep satisfying the demands of the financial markets?

EBay's community can be rebellious when it needs to be. It was outraged in September 1999 when eBay floated on the stock exchange and casually failed to financially reward its precious community with pre-IPO stock. One angry eBayer, who liked to call Whitman, "Miss MBA," described that moment as a turning point in eBay's philosophy. "Meg changed us from a community into a commodity," she said.[88]

The community rebels when decisions are made by eBay management without consultation and when new unpopular policies are implemented. In the summer of 2006, a hike in fees and reduced visibility for shop fronts led to uproar. Like all perceived small changes at eBay, it represented a big deal to members of the community because it affected their livelihoods.

Across the world in August 2006, many powersellers went on strike. The chat rooms crackled with angry comments and promises to sell goods at St. Elsewhere, a code name for competition. Some of them have changed their signatures to: "Welcome to the Fee Bay! *Land of the Fee, Home of the Slave!*" But where can the community go when eBay can provide so many buyers?

Some angry powersellers petitioned Google to launch a rival site and inject some competition into a market dominated by eBay. They have created a Google Group called "Google we need an auction site!" One user, who calls himself "ebayslaveworker" begs: "Please Google! Get this 800 pound gorilla monopoly off our backs."

What would a Google auction mean? Google is one rival that eBay is understandably a little wary of. While eBay has attempted to redress the power balance by forming a close relationship with Yahoo, Google is beginning to step on its toes. EBay can only hope that its feedback system will work like a sticky magnet and protect it from competition.

The global search engine has launched its own payment system called Google Checkout rivalling PayPal. Industry experts suggest it's only a matter of time before it launches an auction. After all, Google is not a brand afraid to innovate.

A number of eBay's savvier powersellers are buying key search terms on Google to drive potential shoppers direct to their own websites, bypassing eBay. Buyers are also using Google, rather than eBay, to connect directly with sellers. Admittedly, Google's search results send a lot of traffic to eBay, but the relationship is imbalanced. Berkeley's Haas School of Business has estimated that around 12 percent of eBay's revenues come indirectly from Google, whereas Google gets only 3 percent of its revenues from eBay.

A decision by Google to hold a party in the middle of eBay Live 2007 prompted a furious face-off between the two companies. EBay announced it was pulling its advertising from Google's AdWords network in the US – worth around $25m annually. Google hurriedly cancelled its party. It won't be the last confrontation between the two.

In the past, Whitman and Omidyar have spoken of the importance of listening to the members. When they don't, they admit, is when they make their biggest mistakes. This time, the community wants the online marketplace to return to its roots and give priority to individuals again.

EBay's community will continue to rebel. New CEO, John Donahoe's raft of changes to help eBay catch up with the changing world have not been popular with sellers who organized a global boycott on May 1 2008.

Some of the community say they have lost faith in the marketplace and that they're disillusioned with the site that once used to mean everything. So is this another blip, another rebellion, like all the others in the past? Will it be resolved once eBayers realize there's nowhere else to go, and that things aren't so bad after all? Or could this be the beginning of the end?

It's an ongoing conundrum for eBay. How can it nurture its community as it grows and grows? Who should eBay really represent – the buyers or the sellers in its community?

Meg Whitman has summed it up: "At its core, eBay is not about auctions. Auctions are an enabler. Auctions make it fun. But eBay is really about a unique sense of community that eBay users are creating for themselves. Can eBay get big while staying small?"[89]

As eBay straddles the world, parts of its community have stopped believing the impossible. They sense that feeling small in the big, big world of eBay is no longer likely. But eBay needs its community. It's the entrepreneurial effort of its army of traders and their desire to make their auctions a success that drives the growth of eBay. They form the basis of its highly effective, profitable business model.

It's the community that do all the hard work. They do the listing, the packing, the posting, the marketing. They make suggestions to guide eBay's innovation. Meanwhile, all eBay needs to do is provide the arena for its market traders to set up their stall.

EBay's future is dependent on its Greek chorus, its community. And as long as management continually takes their pulse and monitors their temperature, the health of the marketplace will be maintained.

EBay is their workplace, their warehouse, their bank, their café, their post room and their telephone service. And that's why eBay's future success depends on its willingness to listen and respond to its community's needs.

EBay has changed our world. It has taught us to think the best of people. It has taught us that anyone can be an entrepreneur; and that individuals can compete in a global marketplace against large corporations. It has showed us that nearly 250 million people will trust a stranger.

EBay has taught us that a human soul is worth just $504 and is less valuable than a toasted cheese sandwich in the image of the

Virgin Mary. And it has made us dream of reaching for a red shooting star.

What other brands can learn from eBay?

◎ EBay is a new kind of brand. It comes from the new generation where brands are less about consistency and more about consumer involvement and community.

◎ EBay is a courageous, gutsy brand. It means that eBay has times when it faces its customers' fierce wrath, but also moments when it can share their joy.

◎ EBay with its emphasis on interaction, involvement, personal experience, culture and community is the shape of brands of the future. When it works best, it is brand as translator, never dictator.

◎ EBay's most successful moments happen when it translates its community guidance into an improved buying and selling experience.

◎ EBay understands the importance of listening to its consumers because they live the experience.

Endnotes

1 Business Week/Interbrand annual ranking of the best global brands, August 18, 2006
2 "Happy 10th Birthday eBay," *Daily Express,* September 5, 2005
3 ebay.co.uk
4 AC Nielsen, 2006
5 "eBay: Money for Old Rope?," *The Money Programme,* BBC2, February 25, 2005
6 Robert D. Hof, "Q&A with eBay's Pierre Omidyar," *Business Week,* December 3, 2001
7 Michelle Conlin with Robert D. Hof, "The eBay Way," *Business Week,* November 29, 2004
8 ibid.
9 Adam Cohen, *The Perfect Store: Inside eBay* (Little, Brown and Company, 2002), p. 16
10 ibid., p. 17
11 ibid.
12 "eBay: Money for Old Rope?," op. cit.
13 Robert D. Hof, op. cit.
14 Kevin Maney, "10 years ago, eBay changed the world, sort of by accident," *USA Today*, March 22, 2005
15 Adam Cohen, op. cit., p. 29
16 ibid., p. 31
17 ibid., p. 40
18 ebay.com
19 Adam Cohen, op. cit., p. 27
20 Robert D. Hof, op. cit.
21 ibid.
22 ibid.
23 Adam Cohen, op. cit., p. 46
24 ibid., p. 48
25 ibid., p. 57
26 ibid., p. 78
27 ibid., p. 71
28 ibid., p. 72
29 ibid., p. 89
30 ibid., p. 84
31 ibid., p. 96
32 ibid., p. 100
33 Patricia Sellers, "eBay's secret," *Fortune*, October 18, 2004
34 *Fortune,* March 21, 2005
35 Patricia Sellers, op. cit.
36 ibid.
37 Adam Cohen, op. cit., p. 111
38 Linda A. Hill and Maria T. Farkas, "Meg Whitman at eBay, Inc.," *Harvard Business Review,* November 17, 2005, p. 4
39 ibid., p. 5
40 Adam Cohen, op. cit., p. 115
41 Linda A. Hill and Maria T. Farkas, op. cit., p. 5
42 ibid., p. 7
43 ibid., p. 8
44 Mary Meeker, "ebay: Whacking the cover off the ball," Morgan Stanley Dean Witter Research, November 13, 1998
45 *Fortune,* September 1, 2005
46 *Fortune,* March 21, 2005
47 Kevin Maney, op. cit.

48 ebay.com

49 Institute of Directors Convention, United Kingdom, April 2006

50 "Happy 10th Birthday eBay," op. cit.

51 ebay.com

52 ibid.

53 Adam Cohen, op. cit., p. 42

54 ibid., p. 29

55 ibid., p. 35

56 ibid., p. 36

57 Tim Jonze, "Death on MySpace," *Guardian,* May 15, 2006

58 Adam Cohen, op. cit., p. 268

59 *Sunday Telegraph,* Australia, September 4, 2005

60 *Daily Express,* August 13, 2005

61 *Daily Star,* August 28, 2005

62 Adam Cohen, op. cit., p. 158

63 ibid.

64 ibid. p. 197

65 Ken Belson with Robert D. Hof and Ben Elgin, "How Yahoo! Japan beat eBay at its own game," *Business Week,* June 4, 2001

66 "The 2002 E.BIZ 25," *Business Week,* October 1, 2002

67 Clay Chandler, "An upstart takes on mighty eBay," *Fortune,* November 15, 2004

68 Interview transcript: Meg Whitman, June 18, 2006, FT.com

69 Adam Cohen, op. cit., p. 229

70 Interview transcript: Meg Whitman, op. cit.

71 ibid.

72 ibid.

73 ibid.

74 Dan Glaister, "A brush with the law," *Guardian,* August 2, 2006

75 Sarah McCartney, *The Fake Factor: Why we love brands but buy fakes* (Cyan Books, 2006)

76 Tom Rawstorne, "Is your eBay bag a fake?," *Daily Mail,* July 4, 2005

77 *Fortune,* May 26, 2003

78 ibid.

79 ibid.

80 Adam Cohen, op. cit., p. 310

81 Linda A. Hill and Maria T. Farkas, op. cit.

82 *Sunday Telegraph,* op. cit.

83 R.M. Ellis and A.J. Haywood, "The implications of eBay for 'real networks': The distribution of goods, money flows and the Internet infrastructure of e-commerce," Chimera working paper number 2006-08, University of Essex

84 "eBay: Money for Old Rope?," op. cit.

85 Elizabeth Day, "Charity shops lose out as second-hand goods go to Internet auctions," *Daily Telegraph,* August 15, 2004

86 *Charity Finance,* September 2005

87 Linda A. Hill and Maria T. Farkas, op. cit., p. 218

88 Said by Rosalinda Baldwin from the Auction Guild in Adam Cohen, op. cit., p. 218

89 Linda A. Hill and Maria T. Farkas, op. cit.

Bibliography

Adam Cohen, *The Perfect Store: Inside eBay* (Little, Brown and Company, 2002)

R.M. Ellis and A.J. Haywood, "The implications of eBay for 'real networks': The distribution of goods, money flows and the Internet infrastructure of e-commerce," Chimera working paper number 2006-08, University of Essex

Linda A. Hill and Maria T. Farkas, "Meg Whitman at eBay, Inc.," *Harvard Business Review*, November 17, 2005

Robert D. Hof, "Q&A with eBay's Pierre Omidyar," *Business Week,* December 3, 2001

Kevin Maney, "10 years ago, eBay changed the world, sort of by accident," *USA Today*, March 22, 2005

Patricia Sellers, "eBay's Secret," *Fortune*, October 18, 2004

"eBay: Money for Old Rope?," *The Money Programme*, BBC2, February 25, 2005

Interview transcript: Meg Whitman, June 18, 2006, FT.com

About the author

Elen Lewis is a freelance writer. She is the editor of The Marketing Society's monthly magazine *Think* and works as a writer and consultant for business. The former editor of *Brand Strategy*, she also writes for magazines and newspapers including the *Financial Times, Independent* and *Guardian*. Her first book *Great Ikea!: A brand for all the people*, was listed in the top five business books of the year by *The Times* in 2005 and has since been published in the US, China, Sweden, Spain, Turkey, Korea and Japan. She also wrote a chapter in *The Bard & Co: Shakespeare's role in modern business*. Elen studied at Oxford University, receiving an MA in English Literature.

You can contact Elen via *www.elenlewis.com*